DIALOGUE
in foreign language education

DIALOGUE
in foreign language education

Edited by
Monika Kusiak

Wydawnictwo Uniwersytetu Jagiellońskiego

Książka dofinansowana przez Uniwersytet Jagielloński ze środków Wydziału Filologicznego oraz Nauczycielskiego Kolegium Języków Obcych

RECENZENT
Prof. dr hab. Hanna Komorowska

PROJEKT OKŁADKI
Agnieszka Winciorek

REDAKTOR
Dorota Węgierska

KOREKTA
Agata Czuj

SKŁAD I ŁAMANIE
Hanna Wiechecka

Wydanie I, Kraków 2009

ISBN 978-83-233-2622-9

WYDAWNICTWO UNIWERSYTETU JAGIELLOŃSKIEGO
www.wuj.pl

Wydawnictwo Uniwersytetu Jagiellońskiego
Redakcja: ul. Michałowskiego 9/2, 31-126 Kraków
tel. (012) 631-18-80, tel./fax (012) 631-18-83
Dystrybucja: ul. Wrocławska 53, 30-011 Kraków
tel. (012) 631-01-97, tel./fax (012) 631-01-98
tel. kom. 0506-006-674, e-mail: sprzedaz@wuj.pl
Konto: PEKAO SA, 80 1240 4722 1111 0000 4856 3325

Contents

Preface

It is with great pleasure that I welcome readers to this collection of papers. The book has benefited from the contribution of several researchers from Poland and abroad. In recent years, most of them have cooperated with the Research Group of the Foreign Language Teacher Training College at the Jagiellonian University. Several of the papers were presented at a seminar which explored different aspects of dialogue in foreign language education organized by the college in May 2007.

The aim of the publication is to stimulate discussion about the multifaceted nature of foreign language education and the interplay between the various factors influencing foreign language learning and teaching. Recently, we have observed a growth in the popularity of the concept of dialogue. Scholars from diverse backgrounds, such as psychology, philosophy or education, have investigated their notion of dialogue.

As editor of this publication, I suggested that the following perspectives of dialogue be explored in relation to foreign language learning:

- an intrapersonal perspective, i.e. the dialogic nature of foreign language learning – processes internal to the learner;
- an interpersonal perspective, e.g. the interaction between learners and the teacher;
- a dialogue within the institution or between several institutions, e.g. cooperation of teachers with various stakeholders;
- a dialogue between various disciplines and approaches in teaching and researching.

I invited writers to comment on the following aspects of dialogue:

- the form of dialogue, e.g. different techniques applied by learners and teachers;
- the subject of dialogue, e.g. linguistic competence, intercultural competence, attitudes;
- the effectiveness of dialogue, e.g. a sense of success in learning and teaching;
- the roles of participants in dialogue, e.g. how learners and teachers construct their roles;
- the range of dialogue, e.g. dialogue between learners, between the teacher and learners, and between the school and learners.

The publication addresses the diversity of the issues mentioned above. Anna Niżegorodcew presents her reflections on a dialogic forum organized at the 2006 Polish Neophilological Society conference. She explores the nature of academic discourse as constructed by the conference participants.

The next two papers focus on developing intercultural communication. Firstly, Lucyna Aleksandrowicz-Pędich discusses intra-cultural aspects of dialogue during intercultural activities; she demonstrates how intercultural studies can facilitate a better understanding of one's own culture. Secondly, Dorota Owczarek looks at the idea of dialogue as developed by Bakhtin in exploring the philosophical foundations underpinning intercultural communication and education.

The next two authors view dialogue as verbal interaction of foreign language learners. Joanna Rokita-Jaśkow discusses the role of parent-child interaction in the development of foreign language communicative abilities of young learners. Agnieszka Nowicka explores the question of how interaction participants construe their situated identities in dialogues in English, and looks at the role of the teacher in this process.

Liljana Skopinskaja and Monika Kusiak report on studies that investigate foreign language reading. Skopinskaja discusses the essence of critical reading through the perspective of dialogic interaction between reader and text, as well as between the target culture and the students' own culture. Kusiak reports on the think-aloud study, investigating how advanced learners read in their native and foreign languages. She focuses on a dialogue between the think-aloud methodology and the construct that the study explores, i.e. reading.

The next three papers deal with the role of information and communication technology in foreign language education. Leszek Bajkowski presents an overview of dialogue systems in the field of human-computer interaction. Jarosław Krajka describes the process of dialogue among students, teachers and industry representatives during the development of the information technology curriculum at the teacher training institution. Magdalena Szczyrbak discusses the role of students and the teacher in student-teacher dialogue in Web-enhanced foreign language learning.

In the last contribution, Vita Kalnberzina presents the results of a study which measures the level of anxiety during foreign language learning, and the impact of this on exam performance. She explores whether it is factors of an intrapersonal character or those of an interpersonal character that are most influential in learners' test performance.

Keeping in mind the topic of the publication, as editor I intended to create a context within which researchers are able to exchange views in a dialogic encounter with other scholars. I believe that "real" dialogue requires the roles of both a participant and an observer. To achieve this, I invited the authors of the papers and other scholars to comment on the contributions in this publication. I assumed that this form of dialogue could facilitate an awareness among the authors of their own assumptions and perhaps more importantly enrich their research with new meanings.

I believe that the polyphony of voices presented in this publication will illustrate to readers that it is only by facing a diversity of perspectives that can we create a more complete, though not a less complex, picture of foreign language education. I hope that the book will inspire readers to ask questions and pursue new paths along "old, well known" themes concerning foreign language education.

I would like to express my gratitude to those who helped me with developing this book. I would like to thank Prof. Anna Niżegorodcew for her continuous encouragement and support. I am grateful to Prof. Lucyna Aleksandrowicz-Pędich for her valuable suggestions concerning the form of the publication. The publication could not have been produced without financial support of Prof. Zofia Berdychowska, Dean of the Faculty of Philology of the Jagiellonian University and Dr. Janusz Król, Head of the Foreign Language Teacher Training College, Jagiellonian University.

Monika Kusiak

Anna Niżegorodcew
Uniwersytet Jagielloński
Kraków

Foreign language teachers in dialogue

1. Introduction

The dialogue referred to in the title of this article concerns the 2006 Polish Neophilological Society (PNS) conference in Kraków (11–13 September 2006) *Dydaktyka języków obcych na początku XXI wieku* [Foreign language teaching at the beginning of the 21st century]. The Society is the only multilingual foreign language teachers' organization in Poland which provides a dialogic forum for an exchange of ideas and opinions in its annual conferences[1]. The 2006 conference was mainly devoted to evaluation and assessment in foreign language teaching. Apart from the main focus, other papers concerning foreign language teaching and learning were also presented during the conference. The conference language was Polish because the speakers were Polish teachers of English, German, French, Russian, Italian, Spanish, and marginally, Polish as a second language[2]. The aim of the following analysis is comparing different approaches of the conference participants to academic discourse focused on foreign language learning and teaching.

My claim is that different traditions linked with academic discourse in foreign language teaching in different countries and academic settings have their impact on the theoretical approaches, methods of research and ways of presentation of seemingly similar topics. What follows is a diversity in the treatment of knowledge, attitudes towards listeners and readers, as well as global versus local approaches to the language of communication and relevant literature. Foreign language teachers in Poland, on the one hand, are influenced by target language traditions but, on the other hand, they create their own approaches on the basis of local situations and problems.

Such differences could be an inspiring source of richness in dialogic encounters. However, it may also happen that authors and their audience do not accept authors coming from other traditions and they put up, consciously or subconsciously, mental barriers, which can be seen in using a specific discourse, characteristic only of a particular tradition, and relying exclusively on the target language models. In such cases there is

---

1 *Foreign language* is usually acquired/learned only in the classroom, in the countries where it is not spoken as a first language, e.g. English is a foreign language in Poland.

2 Those different foreign languages are referred to as *target languages*.

no dialogue between diverse ideas. Conversely, each academic tradition and discourse is closed in its own world and immune to enriching mutual influences.

2. Diversity as a strength and as a weakness

Let us define academic discourse as the discourse of academic communities focused on particular academic disciplines. In the case of foreign language teachers, relevant academic disciplines encompass non-native language learning, teaching and use. These broad disciplines can be subdivided into narrower theoretical and practical areas of interest, among others, theory of second language acquisition vs. theory of foreign language learning, assessment of foreign language learners' and users' competence/proficiency, language teaching policy, new technologies in language teaching, evaluation of foreign language syllabuses and materials, developing language learners' autonomy, evaluation of the foreign language teaching and learning process, new language teaching techniques, teaching foreign languages to young and very young learners and second/foreign language teacher education and development. Obviously, this list can be further expanded. The above areas of interest have all been present in the papers given during the PNS 2006 conference.

According to Zalewski, academic discourse is used by the academic community "for functions related to knowledge-making and knowledge-proliferating mission of that community" (Zalewski, 2004: 177). Let us try to focus on academic discourse in foreign language teaching from the perspective of knowledge-making and knowledge-proliferating in the multilingual world. My claim is that the diversity of the academic discourse in foreign language teaching has its own strengths and weaknesses.

Different approaches do not preclude the mission of knowledge-making and knowledge-proliferating. In fact, new foreign language teaching theories and practices are developed thanks to tensions and controversies between diverse approaches, which are inseparable aspects of development.

However, some basic assumptions and principles, as well as conventions of academic discourse are necessary in academic interactions. We must talk to somebody who will listen to us and will try to understand us. In other words, academic discourse assumes a degree of common knowledge and common discourse conventions.

Traditional academic discourse aims at objectivity and personal detachment from the subject, which is manifested in language use, e.g. the personal pronoun *I* is avoided and the passive voice is preferred. Discipline boundaries in traditional academic discourse are clearly stated. Conversely, in contemporary interdisciplinary academic discourse, boundaries are blurred and personal and contextualized points of view are emphasized. Foreign language teaching is a typical interdisciplinary field. Its source disciplines, to mention only the most important ones, encompass linguistics, psychology, sociology, pedagogy, communication studies, management studies, as well as a multi-faceted area of culture studies.

Let us enumerate some reasons for foreign language teaching academic discourse diversity. Firstly, foreign language teachers' discourse relies more or less heavily on the authorities or on the teachers' own expertise and experience. It seems evident that foreign language teachers' knowledge manifested in their academic discourse, is not only delivered to them by knowledge-makers from the above mentioned academic disciplines but it is also co-constructed by language teachers themselves. Such a participatory approach is present, first of all, in writing courses, where social constructivist theory and critical pedagogy have had great impact on language teaching practitioners for a considerable period of time (see Larsen-Freeman, 1995).

Secondly, foreign language teaching discourse in plenary and session papers and in discussions following presentations and panel discussions can be differently structured and presented. The dialogic aspects of academic discourse are enhanced in the papers which have a clear structure and delivery, as well as when oral presentations are supported by visual aids (handouts, power point presentations), which aim at making the presentations more accessible to the audience. The dialogic character of presentations is also emphasized by frequent eye-contacts with the audience.

On the other hand, dialogue in academic discourse can be jeopardized owing to traditionally hierarchical "top-down" nature of academic communication. Academics have been traditionally used to giving lectures, in which students' questions and feedback were not taken into consideration. Similarly, conference organizers and presenters may leave too little time for discussions following presentations. Listeners are frequently intimidated, especially on a forum where they are supposed to speak in a non-native language. Speakers may also use register and stylistic devices which exclude "others", such as, e.g. using very specialist vocabulary, including difficult terminology and making an impression that what they say is so well-known to professionals that it would be a sign of unprofessionalism to ask for clarification. Chair persons in conference sessions are able to skilfully manage discussions in such a way that questions taken by the presenters are limited to those asked by the participants who the chair persons can recognize as well-known professionals. Summing up, dialogue at conferences is frequently endangered by undemocratic behaviour of those involved in academic discourse.

It seems that the dialogic aspects of presentations were also partly neglected for organizational and psychological reasons at the 2006 PNS conference: under time pressure and due to the presenters' lack of empathy and the participants' reluctance to take part in the discussions.

Finally, diversity stems from the language of communication. There is no consensus on one language of international communication. Although in the world of global communication, facilitated by the Internet, English has doubtlessly become a language of international communication in business, science and technology, teachers of other European languages, such as, e.g. French, frequently resist the dominance of English, relying to a great extent only on the sources written in their target language or translated into it. The same may be the case with teachers of English (as well as with English native speakers), who do not perceive any necessity to learn and use other languages. This attitude may reflect a degree of arrogance but more frequently it is an evidence of a narrow specialization in only one foreign language.

Teachers of less popular languages, such as, e.g. Polish, are used to the fact that they attend conferences and read literature in languages other than Polish. Paradoxically, a dialogue between teachers of less popular languages through English as a language of international communication might be more feasible than a dialogue between a teacher of French and a teacher of English, in particular in a situation when each of them would like to adhere to their own target language and the literature written exclusively in that language.

A conclusion which can be drawn from the above remarks is that academic discourse of foreign language teachers is not uniform due to diverse treatments of knowledge, presenters' approaches and target language traditions.

3. An analysis of academic discourse in the 2006 PNS conference papers

Let us analyse the conference topics and ways of their presentation from the dialogic perspective. Paradoxically, written versions of the conference presentations can provide a better opportunity for foreign language teachers to share ideas with other members of their profession than oral presentations. Teachers can have more time to get acquainted with the presented ideas and practical solutions and to confront them with their teaching practice. The dialogic perspective may refer to various oral and written comments made by foreign language teachers as a follow-up to other teachers' papers. It may also refer to various professional uses of the published papers by foreign language teachers and teacher-trainees.

In the following part of this paper I will focus on the 2006 conference topics and the way of their presentation as they were submitted to the editors to be published in the conference proceedings[3].

The following analysis is based on 69 papers which have been or will be included in two volumes of the conference proceedings and in an issue of *Neofilolog*.

3.1. Roles played by the authors

The majority of the conference papers begin with definitions. Such an approach is common in academic discourse and distinguishes it from everyday discourse, in which people do not need to define things they talk about. The definitions refer to such conference topics, as multilingualism, bilingual competence, pragmatic competence, learner evaluation, etc. Other papers start with emphasizing problems the authors perceive in foreign language teaching, such as new developments in evaluation, developing teachers' and learners' autonomy, content and language integrated teaching, etc.

As has been said before, academic conference discourse combines both types of knowledge: a knowledge constructed by the authors themselves and/or based on other authors' works, and a knowledge co-constructed in discussions and workshops by the audience.

---

[3] The first volume of the 2006 PNS conference proceedings *Dydaktyka języków obcych na początku XXI wieku* has been published in 2007 (Jodłowiec and Niżegorodcew, 2007). The second volume is forthcoming. A few papers will be published in *Neofilolog*.

In the papers submitted for publication, their authors' preferences for different treatments of knowledge can also be discerned. Interestingly, some well-known authors present broad surveys of their topics based on literature (e.g. Zawadzka-Bartnik, 2007), others take on the roles of authorities themselves by presenting their own classifications, categorizations and models (e.g. Wilczyńska, 2007), still others rely on their own teaching experience (e.g. Siek-Piskozub and Strugielska, 2007), and, finally, a few authors follow a clearly structured academic paper model, which combines a literature survey and one's own research (e.g. Cieślicka, 2007).

What makes some authors choose a survey of literature type of paper, and what makes other authors draw more on one's own expertise and experience? It seems that the authors take on different roles in dialogue with their audience: the role of a reviewer (Zawadzka-Bartnik), the role of a theorist (Wilczyńska), the role of a creative teacher (Siek-Piskozub and Strugielska) and the role of a researcher (Cieślicka). Since each of them is a professor in foreign language teaching and they could choose their paper types, probably the roles have been chosen according to their personal preferences.

Such a diversity of approaches presented by the above mentioned representatives of the academic foreign language teaching profession in Poland is also characteristic of other authors whose papers are included in the proceedings. Some of them have chosen topics based on their own research (e.g. teaching vocabulary – Otwinowska-Kasztelanic, 2007; developing learners' autonomy and multilingualism – Pawlak, 2007), others presented surveys of theory and research based on literature (e.g. Ewert, 2007; Bromberek-Dyzman, 2007; Kubiczek forthcoming) or, most frequently, they drew on their own teaching experience, presenting new technologies, experiments and teaching suggestions, for instance, an interesting group of papers focused on e-learning (e.g. Widła, 2007; Krajka forthcoming). Thus, similarly to the former group of authors, other writers can also be classified according to the roles they play: of researchers, reviewers or creative teachers.

3.2. Authors as researchers

Let us pay special attention to one of the above mentioned roles – the one of researchers. Out of 69 papers there are 24 articles which focus primarily or partly on language learning and teaching research conducted by the authors.

The research studies are concerned first of all with various aspects of evaluation and assessment, although there are also a few studies focused on other problems, such as students' awareness of similarities between languages (Otwinowska-Kasztelanic, 2007) or understanding metaphors and idioms (Cieślicka, 2007; Sułkowska forthcoming).

On the basis of an analysis of the research topics, research methods, research subjects and types of presentation, the following conclusions can be drawn. Firstly, evaluation and assessment as the main conference topics seem to have been interesting for a great number of the authors. It is a multi-faceted theme and, accordingly, it has been approached from different perspectives: teacher assessment, student assessment, peer assessment, self-evaluation, evaluation of teaching materials, evaluation of methods of assessment, etc.

Secondly, opinion surveys were the most popular method of research used by the researchers, e.g. Pawlak, 2007; Jarząbek forthcoming. A few studies were based on didactic experiments, e.g. Otwinowska-Kasztelanic, 2007. The remaining studies most frequently involved teachers' action research and case studies. Research subjects as a rule were university or school students and teachers. The authors frequently presented pilot studies or studies being part of larger projects.

Finally, the analyses and discussions of results were rather modest and they indicated that, except for a few experienced researchers, the remaining writers are first of all teachers and teacher trainers with very little experience in language learning and teaching research. The question arises how to educate language teachers and language teacher trainers to professionally design, conduct and present their research studies. It seems that a course in research design, including statistics for language studies, should be an indispensable component of undergraduate and graduate students' education.

3.3. Dialogue with readers in conference papers

The dialogic character of research papers is closely linked with a more general question of the treatment of readers by the authors. The question arises what should be an ideal presentation of one's topic, that is, a presentation which would enable readers to follow the authors' ideas as closely as possible.

The first observation that should be made is that the readers are not a homogenous group, which affects their treatment by the authors. The papers included in the conference proceedings have been intended not only for experienced language teaching lecturers, researchers and graduate students. They have been also intended for less experienced readers, school teachers and undergraduate students. Such a diversity is in line with the philosophy and mission of the Polish Neophilological Society, which is to link a theoretical and a practical side of the foreign language teaching profession. Yet, the authors are also a heterogeneous group as far as their sophistication and experience level is concerned. Some of them probably are not aware of the intricacies of stylistic and conventional matters in academic writing.

The second observation refers to the clarity of exposition. The question is obviously linked with the structure of the papers. In comparison with clearly structured academic papers published in renowned journals, the majority of the 2006 PNS conference papers are much more awkwardly structured. The question arises if the less experienced authors have known that their aims should be explicitly stated and the topical ideas highlighted.

In fact, only some authors clearly formulate their aims in presenting their views and research. For instance, Cieślicka (2007: 65) writes: "Niniejszy artykuł ma na celu analizę psycholingwistycznych badań nad językiem metaforycznym" [the aim of this article is to analyse research on metaphorical language][4]. Similarly, Michońska-Stadnik (2007: 57) formulates her aim: "celem tego artykułu jest krótkie zaprezentowanie najciekawszych osiągnięć w najnowszych badaniach dotyczących przyswajania i przechowywania słownictwa w pamięci" [the aim of this article is a short presentation of the

[4] This author's translations.

most interesting results in the most recent research on lexical acquisition and storage of lexicon in memory]. Also only a few authors begin their papers by presenting their content (e.g. Wilczyńska writes "omówię kolejno trzy aspekty: wielojęzyczność jako zjawisko współczesne, pojęcie kompetencji wielojęzycznej i rozwijanie tej kompetencji" [three consecutive aspects will be discussed: multilingualism as a modern phenomenon, the concept of multilingual competence and development of multilingual competence].

As far as the treatment of topics is concerned, some approaches seem inherently easier than others. The presentation of a model is more difficult than detailed exemplifications based on case studies. A few graphical models accompanying the papers may be difficult to be followed without interpretation and examples, e.g. Chudak (2007). Workshop type papers illustrated with examples of discourse samples or tasks are more reader-friendly for teachers, e.g. Paprocka-Piotrowska (2007), Rokita-Jaśkow (2007).

Last but not least, one of the papers stands in sharp contrast to all other papers – in a plenary lecture Sławek (2007) asked a question belonging to theory and philosophy of literature "czy literatura pomaga nam być razem?" [does literature help us be together]. Obviously, such a philosophical question and its treatment in the paper is not reader-friendly in the sense of providing readers with ready answers to their professional problems. However, attempts to clarify the question on the basis of literary works show the author's deep respect for the readers, who are invited to co-construct the meanings of the author's implicit and allusive answers through their own unique experience with literature.

3.4. Background knowledge and language of communication

Diversity in the papers also stems from the authors' knowledge of the subject matter and the target language/languages. Although Polish as the conference language has facilitated communication between teachers of different target languages, it has not removed differences in the approaches between teachers of English, French and German. Their papers show that their background knowledge has been first of all shaped by the theoretical approaches and research studies developed in the target language countries and/or by the target language theorists in Poland. A majority of the teachers make references only to the target language literature. On the other hand, if they refer to books and articles in another language, it is as a rule the English language. Thus, in spite of what has been said before about the reluctance of other European speakers to use English as a language of international communication, it seems that English has already attained such a status in language learning and teaching.

As a consequence of the privileged position of English language theorists in the field of foreign language learning and teaching, the latest developments in the field are most frequently published first in English, to be only later translated and made known to the teaching profession in other languages. It seems that academic teachers of other languages should be aware of that fact. Otherwise, as it has happened in a few papers given at the 2006 PNS conference, their authors "re-discover" in other languages theories and research studies which were first described many years ago in the original English versions. Such papers may be very useful in teacher training, yet they have a downgrading effect in an academic conference.

Academic communication requires efficiency. Both knowledge-making and knowledge-proliferating require efficient communication and common background knowledge. It seems that teachers of foreign languages who ignore English literature in language learning and teaching do a disservice to their profession. Diversity should not mean ignorance.

4. Conclusion

In conclusion, the diversity of the academic discourse as evidenced in the papers presented at the 2006 PNS conference may have positive and negative sides. The positive aspects involve the diversity of roles. The different roles the authors play enrich the readers' knowledge and provide them with inspiration for their own research and teaching. Writers in the roles of researchers, reviewers, theorists and creative teachers can all find interested readers among foreign language teachers and teacher-trainees. They can be also inspiring for one another.

As far as the conference topics are concerned, "dialogue of papers" in the sense of a great number of papers focused on the main conference topic – assessment and evaluation, has been successful and provided multi-faceted approaches. Another conference topic – multilingualism, has been much less popular.

On the other hand, "diverse" may mean "less valuable". In that other sense, negative aspects of diversity can be observed in an unclear structure and presentation of the papers, as well as in poorly designed and described research studies.

The question of the language of communication is open to discussion. However, it seems unquestionable that the latest developments in the field of foreign language learning and teaching are published in English. Ignoring them due to a negative attitude to the English language or inability to read in English is also a negative aspect of diversity. In consequence, one target language teachers tend to communicate only in a closed circle, even if the conference language, like in PNS conferences, is the first language of the conference participants. What seems to be necessary in order to develop an enriching dialogue of teachers teaching different foreign languages is their common knowledge of recent advancements in theory and research in the field of second/foreign language learning and teaching, as well as their willingness to communicate with teachers of different foreign languages.

Bibliography

Bromberek-Dyzman, K., 2007, "Intencjonalność a interjęzykowa kompetencja pragmatyczna", [in:] M. Jodłowiec, A. Niżegorodcew, eds, *Dydaktyka języków obcych na początku XXI wieku*, Kraków: Wydawnictwo Uniwersytetu Jagiellońskiego, pp. 87–98.

Cieślicka, A., 2007, "Kompetencja metaforyczna w języku obcym: rola metafor pojęciowych w przetwarzaniu języka obcego", [in:] M. Jodłowiec, A. Niżegorodcew, eds, *Dydaktyka języków obcych na początku XXI wieku*, Kraków: Wydawnictwo Uniwersytetu Jagiellońskiego, pp. 65–75.

Chudak, S., 2007, "Ewaluacja podręczników do nauki języków obcych pod kątem treści wspierających autonomię uczniów dorosłych", [in:] M. Jodłowiec, A. Niżegorodcew, eds, *Dydaktyka języków obcych na początku XXI wieku*, Kraków: Wydawnictwo Uniwersytetu Jagiellońskiego, pp. 211–222.

Ewert, A., 2007, "Próba identyfikacji zmiennych wpływających na rozwój kompetencji bilingwalnej", [in:] M. Jodłowiec, A. Niżegorodcew, eds, *Dydaktyka języków obcych na początku XXI wieku*, Kraków: Wydawnictwo Uniwersytetu Jagiellońskiego, pp. 41–53.

Jarząbek, A., forthcoming, *O nastawieniu nauczycieli do samooceny uczących się.*

Krajka, J., forthcoming, *Ewaluacja efektów kształcenia w platformach nauczania na odległość.*

Kubiczek, A., forthcoming, *L1, L2, L3,... LN – o problemach wielojęzyczności i definiowania języków.*

Larsen-Freeman, D., 1995, "On the changing role of linguistics in the education of second language teachers: Past, present and future", [in:] J. Alatis, C. Straehle, B. Gallenberger, M. Ronkin, eds, *Georgetown University Round Table on Languages and Linguistics*, Washington, DC: Georgetown University Press, pp. 711–724.

Michońska-Stadnik, A., 2007, "Uwagi na temat przechowywania w pamięci oraz struktury dwujęzycznych zasobów leksykalnych", [in:] M. Jodłowiec, A. Niżegorodcew, eds, *Dydaktyka języków obcych na początku XXI wieku*, Kraków: Wydawnictwo Uniwersytetu Jagiellońskiego, pp. 57–63.

Otwinowska-Kasztelanic, A., 2007, "Na drodze ku różnojęzyczności: podnoszenie świadomości językowej przy nauczaniu słownictwa na przykładzie języka angielskiego", [in:] M. Jodłowiec, A. Niżegorodcew, eds, *Dydaktyka języków obcych na początku XXI wieku*, Kraków: Wydawnictwo Uniwersytetu Jagiellońskiego, pp. 99–110.

Paprocka-Piotrowska, U., 2007, "Stereotyp w dialogu interkulturowym – wprowadzenie do warsztatu", [in:] M. Jodłowiec, A. Niżegorodcew, eds, *Dydaktyka języków obcych na początku XXI wieku*, Kraków: Wydawnictwo Uniwersytetu Jagiellońskiego, pp. 287–292.

Pawlak, M., 2007, "Rola Europejskiego portfolio językowego dla uczniów szkół ponadgimnazjalnych i studentów w rozwijaniu wielojęzyczności, wielokulturowości i autonomii ucznia", [in:] M. Jodłowiec, A. Niżegorodcew, eds, *Dydaktyka języków obcych na początku XXI wieku*, Kraków: Wydawnictwo Uniwersytetu Jagiellońskiego, pp. 167–179.

Rokita-Jaśkow, J., 2007, "Jak wspierać rozwój umiejętności komunikacji dziecka w języku obcym?", [in:] M. Jodłowiec, A. Niżegorodcew, eds, *Dydaktyka języków obcych na początku XXI wieku*, Kraków: Wydawnictwo Uniwersytetu Jagiellońskiego, pp. 305–316.

Siek-Piskozub, T., A. Strugielska, 2007, "Jak kształcić nauczyciela autonomicznego. Historia pewnego seminarium", [in:] M. Jodłowiec, A. Niżegorodcew, eds, *Dydaktyka języków obcych na początku XXI wieku*, Kraków: Wydawnictwo Uniwersytetu Jagiellońskiego, pp. 337–348.

Sławek, T., 2007, "Nie czujemy się pewni w objaśnianym nam świecie. Czy literatura pomaga nam być razem?", [in:] M. Jodłowiec, A. Niżegorodcew, eds, *Dydaktyka języków obcych na początku XXI wieku*, Kraków: Wydawnictwo Uniwersytetu Jagiellońskiego, pp. 11–24.

Sułkowska, M., forthcoming, *Nauczanie i przyswajanie frazeologizmów w języku obcym.*

Widła, H., 2007, "Nauczanie i ocenianie na platformie kształcenia na odległość", [in:] M. Jodłowiec, A. Niżegorodcew, eds, *Dydaktyka języków obcych na początku XXI wieku*, Kraków: Wydawnictwo Uniwersytetu Jagiellońskiego, pp. 113–123.

Wilczyńska, W., 2007, "Wielojęzyczność – przegląd problematyki w ujęciu dydaktycznym", [in:] M. Jodłowiec, A. Niżegorodcew, eds, *Dydaktyka języków obcych na początku XXI wieku*, Kraków: Wydawnictwo Uniwersytetu Jagiellońskiego, pp. 27–40.

Zalewski, J., 2004, *Epistemology of the Composing Process: Writing in English for General Academic Purposes*, Opole: Wydawnictwo Uniwersytetu Opolskiego.

Zawadzka-Bartnik, E., 2007, "Stare i nowe problemy ewaluacji", [in:] M. Jodłowiec, A. Niżegorodcew, eds, *Dydaktyka języków obcych na początku XXI wieku*, Kraków: Wydawnictwo Uniwersytetu Jagiellońskiego, pp. 155–166.

DISCUSSION

Ewa Bandura
Uniwersytet Jagielloński
Kraków

Speaker's roles and responsibilities in academic discourse

The article provokes further comments on the quality of academic conference presentations. Naturally, our reception of any speaker's presentation is clearly influenced by our expectations. In this sense Prof. Niżegorodcew's article inspires to think of our own assumptions concerning the delivery of conference papers. It helped me to become aware of my own priorities as a college lecturer as well as conference presenter. I had always believed that the aim of lecture and conference papers alike is to inform (making the content accessible) and initiate a discussion (giving food for thought). Clear structure, visual aids (including multimedia) and maintaining contact with the audience, as stated in the article, contribute to the effectiveness of the presentation, which is further confirmed by feedback, including a variety of questions from both experts in the topic and less knowledgeable, but equally attentive, members of the audience. I had assumed this to be a widely acknowledged approach irrespective of an academic discipline represented by the presenter.

Experience proved otherwise. A "monologic" approach seems to be quite a common practice, especially in foreign literature and culture conference sections. What's more, some speakers seem not to distinguish between reading their articles at high speed and giving oral presentations. The reasons of this situation are enumerated in the article and vary from personal preferences and target language traditions to different academic settings. Surprisingly, my own suggestions to some of the conference organisers in Poland, aiming to provide all future speakers with some guidelines as to the format of the presentations, was met with mixed reactions. This made me think not only of the diversity of approaches to academic discourse but also of an indifference to the issue. The article in question made me reflect again on the nature of academic discourse and the role of interlocutors' attitudes in communication.

Anna Kosiarz-Stolarska
Uniwersytet Jagielloński
Kraków

Dialogue between "academic tribes" and "territories"

When I was listening to Prof. Anna Niżegorodcew's paper during the seminar, the first reflection which came to my mind was that although the academic discipline embracing foreign language teaching seems to be relatively homogenous, it is actually diverse. Different target languages and their traditions of teaching determine to a great extent what actually happens in the classroom.

I would like to illustrate this claim with an observation from my recent experience of teaching English to students who major in German in the Foreign Language Teacher Training College. It is important to note that the students learnt English as their second foreign language. When a group of teachers from the English section of the College began to teach the students, we were surprised to hear that the students did not like the course. In fact, the students complained that "they were learning nothing". As a coordinator of the group of the teachers, I felt responsible for the organization of the course and decided to investigate the problem. I did not think that the teachers were the main reason why the students did not like the classes; all of them were experienced professionals. When asked about the main source of their dissatisfaction with the course, the students explained that they expected translation exercises and tests in every class. The communicative way of testing English and the lack of translation exercises made them feel that their language progress was not sufficient. The Grammar-Translation Method the students had been exposed to in their German classes caused the students to treat translation as an indispensable part of successful foreign language learning.

Now I can see a positive aspect of the situation, by which I was originally baffled. I think that being exposed to different methods of teaching a foreign language can be beneficial to future teachers of English and German. Prospective teachers can observe how the different techniques they experience as foreign language students are put into real classroom practice. The methodological diversity that students experience as they learn two foreign languages is very likely to enrich their teaching expertise in their future work. I hope that the exposure to different methods and techniques will initiate the process of reflecting, evaluating and analyzing a complex nature of a foreign language classroom and result in creative teaching in the future.

My second comment concerns the analysis of the dialogue between conference participants Prof. Anna Niżegorodcew presents in her paper. This analysis reminds me of a book which I read some time ago, namely *Academic Tribes and Territories* by Tony Becher (1989, Open University Press). The book discusses the metaphor of academics from various disciplines seen as members of different "academic tribes" and occupying different "academic territories". Although Tony Becher's research concerns the differences between the academic culture of humanities and sciences, I think we can apply this metaphor to describe the different worlds of academic discourse of the conference participants described by Prof. Niżegorodcew. Teachers of different foreign languages belong to different "tribes", each having their distinctive cultures. Problems in the dialogue between members of those different tribes result from differences between those cultures.

Prof. Niżegordcew's paper is an attempt to understand the differences between members of "academic tribes" of different foreign language "territories". Nowadays we can observe that there is no one theory or approach which could be applied to teaching all foreign languages. It is the target language that determines the methodology of teaching it. The reasons for this situation are of social and cultural origin, including, among others, negative attitudes to the privileged position of the English language in foreign language learning and teaching or inability to read in English, as Prof. Niżegorodcew points out.

What should be done to make the dialogue between different "academic" tribes more successful? Summarizing his research Becher says that it should be possible for people in different academic worlds to influence one another. The first step in this dialogue is to accept the depth of the differences. Another step requires understanding those differences. Prof. Niżegorodcew's paper helps us to achieve both aims and in this way to make the academic dialogue more successful and efficient.

Lucyna Aleksandrowicz-Pędich
Szkoła Wyższa Psychologii Społecznej
Warszawa

Intracultural dialogue during intercultural activities

Intercultural and intracultural

Intercultural communication has gained a respected place in academic research, higher education curricula, language teaching and in-service training for various professions. There exists a well-developed intercultural framework, based largely on the work of Edward Hall, Geert Hofstede, Charles Hampden-Turner and Fons Trompenaars. In the field of intercultural studies in language education seminal work has been done by Claire Kramsch and Michael Byram. Intercultural training is provided to learners at special courses, offered at college level, and also during special training sessions at the workplace (especially in the business context), but in practice the main place of intercultural activities is the language classroom. This is where the intercultural component has a chance to reach the largest number of people; the process of teaching foreign languages, especially English, has universally become a component of general education, usually starting at primary level.

Culture and intercultural competence as components of foreign language education seem to raise little doubt among learners and teachers alike.

> Whatever presence culture may have in the language classroom, those who enter the classroom expect culture. They have explicit expectations, expressed perhaps as a wish to learn about the ways and lives of the people who speak the language to be learned, or as a need to know how to behave and how not to behave while among these people. Students expect to receive this information, and teachers expect to teach it. This is the outright cultural act of language teaching/learning set within the cultural environment of the classroom. (Swiderski, 1993: 19)

Thus culture is an unavoidable element in the language classroom. In terms of methodology, language teaching tends to be organized around grammar, vocabulary and skills development. The concept of skills development includes the importance of intercultural competence alongside the traditional four skills of speaking, listening, reading and writing. The notion of socio-cultural competence stresses the importance of cultural awareness and its communicative impact, while documents such as the *Common European Framework* officially indicate the recognition of socio-cultural knowledge, practical skills (social, living, vocational, leisure), intercultural skills (meaning bringing L1 and L2 cultures into relation), as well as the formation of attitudes of openness and interest towards other cultures and their representatives, and a willingness to modify one's perception of cultural differences (Komorowska, 2006: 65–66). The language teacher's role as a cultural mediator, even if sometimes neglected in practice, is recognized in teacher education and promoted in research concerning the teacher's role in the process of foreign language learning (Zawadzka, 2004; Aleksandrowicz-Pędich, 2005; Bandura, 2007). Teacher education, available coursebooks and additional materials encourage the presence of intercultural activities during the language lessons.

An essential component of intercultural activities is intracultural dialogue, be it explicit or implicit. Intercultural studies enhance intracultural perceptions, a better understanding of one's own culture and its diverse patterns. As Samuel Huntington (2002: 129) has pointed out, "identity at any level – personal, tribal, racial, civilizational – can only be defined in relation to an 'other,' a different person, tribe, race or civilization." When learning about the culture of the other, the learner is constantly encouraged to look at his own culture. The process is frequently implicit as the teacher's explicit attention is focused on the components of the target language culture or, as may be the case in the teaching of English, on the idea of the Other and a different culture, in the process of preparing the learner for the use of English as primarily the *lingua franca* of the modern world.

Some intercultural activities involve overt study of one's own culture. The student is then involved in an open intracultural dialogue, although the experience is not always verbalized. However, the mental process of better understanding one's own self and silent reflection in the case of less outspoken students is of equal value to verbalized cultural comparison. The intracultural dialogue approach is the essence of personal sociocultural development.

This article presents several intercultural activities, which are analyzed from the point of view of the intracultural dialogue in which the learners become involved. The dialogue takes place at the level of attention to daily living, social practices, socially accepted behavior, non-verbal communication as well as the value system and national stereotyping. The examples and observations are based on classroom research conducted during my own broad experiences of teaching intercultural activities to students from Poland as well as from other countries. The classroom procedures presented have been designed by myself and practiced in various teaching contexts.

Daily living: "What did you have for breakfast?"

The activity "What did you have for breakfast?" is a good example of an intercultural activity which can already be done at a pre-intermediate (or even elementary) level. It is a simple activity which involves putting the question "What did you have for breakfast?" and eliciting answers from all the students. When the activity is conducted with Polish students, a pattern of Polish breakfast emerges, which tends to be a sandwich with cheese or meat cold slices of meat and tea. However, there are always exceptions to the rule – students who have had scrambled eggs, muesli, yoghurt, coffee only or, on one occasion, a student who would not have breakfast because she regularly attends morning services at church. The other variations concern having breakfast as a family event or eating it on one's own. In the first case breakfast has the function of creating family bonds, in the second it tends to be merely a response to physiological needs. This simple "What did you have for breakfast?" activity makes students realize that there is a national pattern of daily living with reference to the function of breakfast but there are divergences from the pattern. It is an introduction to the awareness of the absence of intracultural homogeneity and the dynamic quality of culture.

A possible follow-up to this activity is asking students what they received for breakfast when they traveled abroad, and whether this was a sample of national cuisine or merely hotel food, or something still different. Food is one of the most disturbing factors when traveling or living abroad. My Chinese students in Warsaw complained about Polish food, but when, during the class break, one of them took out the food which she brought with her, it was indeed discouraging – a cheap sausage and a large, dry roll. It couldn't have tasted nice, but was not representative of Polish cuisine either. It was food which is inexpensive, easily available and convenient as a packed meal.

Food resentment is one of the frequent problems in living abroad. It often comes as a demonstration of a prolonged culture shock, verbalized as "our food is much better than theirs". The remembrance of variations within the national cuisine may serve as a sobering thought that the problems with adjustment to foreign conditions stem from something else than seemingly tasteless food.

Modes of behavior: visits at home

This is a cross-cultural activity which serves as both reading and writing practice and is designed for upper-intermediate learners of English. It begins with a task during which students read two descriptions of stages of a visit in an Arab home and a Jewish home (Shipler, 2002: 349–352). The instructions how to behave cover five stages of a visit: preparations, entrance and sitting down, the conversation, the meal and goodbyes. While reading students are told to focus on similarities and differences of these two neighboring cultures, which constitutes the first important stage of the cross-cultural analysis. Then, in pairs or small groups they are asked to write similar guidelines with reference to their own culture (the groups should be nationally homogeneous). In the next stage of the lesson they are asked to compare the guidelines produced by one group with those prepared by another group. Thus first the students have to negotiate the accepted behavior within small groups, and during the later stage of the class compare the description from their group with those of the others. The activity requires constant intracultural dialogue and finding the common ground with other in-group members. The significance of rules of social etiquette when paying home visits undergoes the intracultural process of negotiations.

One of the inconsistencies in the Polish pattern of entrance and goodbyes is the system of shaking hands. There are several variations which may be troubling if one is brought up according to one system considered to be the standard of good behavior. Do women shake hands with men? In the East of Poland often only men shake hands with each other, ignoring women, who either refrain from any physical contact, or kiss on the cheek. The kissing ritual has no fixed pattern either. Is it twice or three times? Twice with strangers and three times with relatives? Do men kiss each other? It is only if they are relatives? At what level of familiarity do women move from a handshake to a kiss? There are many variations and a lack of an established standard of social etiquette with regard to the handshake and kiss ritual.

Mundane or symbolic: taking off shoes

Taking off shoes upon entering a house is one of the most disputed topics among Poles. Apparently there is no one pattern while at the same time the issue is highly contentious and the ignorance of the host's beliefs about taking off shoes upon entering the house as a visitor may lead to being perceived as rude and having bad manners.

Taking off shoes is required in mosques and this is usually clearly indicated, especially in places where there are a large numbers of tourists who may not be aware of this tradition and requirement. Taking off shoes in a mosque creates a boundary between the profane and the sacred. In private homes the matter is much more complicated. Taking off shoes is often dictated by tradition resulting from the climate (frequent snow and mud) – thus in Iceland and Sweden one is usually expected to take off shoes, and in Switzerland a tray with a grating is provided for these. But taking off shoes is also a symbolic act of crossing the boundary between the public and the private and thus the rule applies even when the snow is nowadays removed efficiently and transportation is done by car from door to door (which is largely the case in both the Nordic countries mentioned). The rule of taking off shoes at the threshold applies to Asian cultures, as described in a fragment which could be used as a teaching device (reading practice) when introducing the topic of whether to take off shoes or not when entering somebody's house:

> The *ŏndol* heating system is one reason why Koreans sit on the floor, sleep on the floor, and work and eat at low tables instead of raised tables with chairs. At night, the few pieces of furniture are pushed to the side and pads and quilts are brought from the closet and unrolled for sleeping, again on the warm floor. The floor in a Korean house therefore is not really a "floor" at all but a special living surface that is constantly being cleaned and polished. Stepping on this surface with shoes on would be like stepping on the sofa or bed with shoes on in an American house. This is why Koreans always leave their shoes outside the room door or underneath the little porch, if there is one. In fact, it feels so unnatural to enter someone's living space with shoes on that even in modern or "Western-style" homes and apartments there is a little entryway designed for taking shoes off and putting them on. (Clark, 2000: 94)

In Poland there is no similar clear rule, but the emotions seem to rise very high when students are asked about their own rules with regard to taking off shoes. Doing it in a home where the hosts do not expect their guests to take off shoes is highly irritating for the hosts. It seems that the further one goes to the east of Poland, the more likely one is to be expected to take off one's shoes, but by no means is this a simple rule. As during their recent history Poles have been moved large distances in Europe, an inhabitant of Wroclaw is likely to have been brought up according to Eastern European traditions. Hence it is difficult to formulate a social rule for this behavior within Poland.

The topic of taking off shoes deals not only with intracultural dialogue, but also the issue of interpersonal communication competence in intracultural settings. Thus its pedagogical value extends beyond the borders of knowing how to behave in some places abroad.

Socially un/acceptable: kissing in public

Another issue which incites heated intracultural discussions among Polish students is kissing in public. A possible methodological approach to this issue comes from an activity "In the Mind of the Beholder" included in *Culture Matters. The Peace Corps Cross-Cultural Workbook* (Storti, no date: 20–24). The activity consists of two parts. Students are given descriptions of several behaviors and are asked to write down their immediate responses to them or their interpretations in terms of their own cultural values, beliefs or perceptions. One of the types of behavior described is "A young man and a young woman are kissing each other while seated on a park bench." In the second part of the activity students are asked to respond to the same behavior considering an additional key description of a different culture. In the case of kissing in public the additional description is "by someone from a culture where men and women never touch in public". Indeed, two Nigerian students in the group which I have taught in Warsaw said that the only possible interpretation of such a behavior in their country would be in terms of mental disturbance of people behaving in this way. Responses of young Polish people to the idea of kissing in public are by no means homogeneous and the issue demonstrates noticeable intragroup variations. The question of whether kissing in public creates heated in-group discussion was evident when I even had a student's reaction which verged on physical distaste, when he vehemently protested against discussing the issue of kissing in public, claiming it to be sickening. This came as a surprise to some other students, so clearly there was no agreement as to whether kissing in public places in Poland is acceptable or not. This topic not only has the value of demonstrating intracultural variations in the perception of such a behavior, but also a pedagogical value with reference to personal behavior. It is definitely useful for some students to learn that kissing in public can be upsetting and irritating for people from their own cultural environment, generally assumed as safe in terms of knowing intuitively what is acceptable and what controversial. Opinion forming is another benefit of this activity.

For purposes of cross-cultural training it is worthwhile making students aware that in some cultures kissing in public may be considered a criminal behavior. An example may come from Arab or Indian cultures:

> Also consider, for example, a report in the 5 October 1997 issue of the popular Indian (English language) magazine *The Week* headlined 'Under the Greenwood Trees ... No more kissing, says Mayor Shakuntula Arya', which is followed by an interview headlined 'We Should Not Tolerate

> Obscenity'. Shakuntula was complaining about young couples kissing in Lodhi Garden, a central park in India's capital city, and seeking a total ban on kissing in public places in Delhi. According to the report, 'Arya believes that public display of affection is an affront to Indian sensibility'. (Birch, Shirato, Srivastava, 2001: 39)

It might be worthwhile to point out to the students that the contention over the issue of kissing in public stems from the discrepancy over this area of behavior within Western culture. "In Colonial days kissing in public was regarded as an abomination, and kissing, even by husband and wife, upon the Sabbath, was a criminal offense" (Train, 1931: 56). Even though Colonial times are long gone, a similar attitude of distaste is likely to occur in some parts of the United States. And yet, it is also there, especially in places such as San Francisco or Greenwich Village in New York, where almost any public display of emotions is acceptable.

Non-verbal behavior: eye contact

Non-verbal behavior is one of the key issues in intercultural training. It involves studying differences in gestures, facial expression, dress code, attitude to nudity, use of public space, proxemics. One of the approaches is to focus on eye contact. Eye contact relates to issues such as modesty, directness and honesty. *The Peace Corps Cross-Cultural Workbook* recommends an activity (Storti, no date: 85) in which students are asked to observe the degree and nature of eye contact in a diversity of situations, such as between two men of the same age, two women of the same age, an older and younger man/woman, between a man and a woman, between a husband and wife when in public, between a boss and an employee, between a teacher and a student, between a parent and a child, and between people passing on the street. In order to involve the students in the intracultural dialogue on this issue it is best to ask them to write down their opinions without consulting the others, and in the second stage of the activity to compare the notes. In general, when teaching about the issue of eye contact is done in an all-Polish group there is relatively little variation in the opinions on the subject. The Icelandic students whom I taught, however, learnt from their Austrian colleague (a student on the exchange programme) that Icelanders, when greeting a new person, look him/her in the eyes only briefly and then tend to look sideways or upon another person in the company, preferably another Icelander. The Icelandic students seemed to be taken by surprise upon hearing this observation. After this revelation I started observing Icelanders more closely when I met new people and indeed there was truth in this observation of the Austrian student. The pedagogical implication of the situation described is that the perception of one's own culture can be enhanced when an external observer is introduced.

Intracultural points of view: "Seven ways to annoy the Scots"

This activity is taken from the book *Focus on Britain* by David Maule (British Council Web Pages) and I first saw it adapted to classroom conditions by a Hungarian colleague of mine, Ildiko Lazar, an expert in intercultural communication. From the language teaching perspective it is an activity which develops reading and speaking skills. The students' first task is to read a list of seven ways to annoy the Scots (which are: use England instead of Britain, British instead of Scottish, Scotch to refer to people, pretend not to have heard of Robert Burns, say it would be better if the UK had one football team instead of four, talk of men wearing skirts and imitate the local accent). The first benefit of this activity is obviously raising the students' awareness about the United Kingdom, and Scotland and the Scots in particular. The follow-up suggested by Ildiko Lazar is to ask the learners to think of seven ways to annoy a Hungarian. With Polish students, the follow-up is to ask them to think of seven ways to annoy a Pole. This is an activity which strongly explores the idea of intracultural dialogue since the students negotiate their own perception by the others on two levels: individual reflection (what irritates me in the attitude of foreigners) and as an in-group discussion (what irritates us as a nation).

The examples suggested by Polish students give rise to concern about the nation's self-image. They tend to be connected with the perception of Poles as abusing alcohol, as thieves and as capable only of doing simple menial jobs. The assumption that Poles speak Russian is another one. Polish students usually fail to grasp the idea of "pretend not to have heard of Robert Burns", the aim of which is really to indicate that each nation has its great and famous representatives. The overall self-image resulting from this activity is of the low national self-esteem of young Poles. The teacher's contribution here may come in the re-working the "Robert Burns" idea by recalling such personalities as Nicolaus Copernicus, Frederic Chopin, Maria Sklodowska-Curie, Joseph Conrad, Roman Polanski or John Paul the Second. "Ay, there's the rub", however: they were all either of mixed origin and/or succeeded abroad.

Values: fate and destiny

Polish perception of fate and destiny may reveal itself in an interesting way in another activity taken from *The Peace Corps Cross-Cultural Workbook*, from the section focusing on the value system. The values are the aspects of culture whose external manifestations are not always explicit. The activity (Storti, no date: 13) involves linking values to behavior, for example "use of understatement" as expressing indirectness, "at a meeting, agreeing with a suggestion you think is wrong" as an expression of the importance of saving face, or "accepting without question that something cannot be changed" as an expression of fatalism. The aim of the activity is to increase the awareness that a specific behavior often has its roots in the system of values and beliefs. Each behavior/value pair can be linked to students' own culture, thus involving them in the intracultural dialogue.

The most surprising aspect of this activity (and an intracultural reflection) is that the overwhelming majority's of the students believe in fatalism as an inherent Polish value. Young Poles do not believe that they are in control of their lives. The most recent history of Poland (successful transformation from political dictatorship to democracy) seems to suggest the nation's ability to influence its own destiny, but interesting intracultural issues are whether this might have changed with the generation or whether the self-determination of Poles is a group phenomenon, while on the individual level Polish national character embodies the Eastern-European fatalism.

The study of one's own value system is best done in comparison with another culture. *The Peace Corps Cross-Cultural Workbook* suggests some interesting ways of looking at the American value system. When the students compare the Polish value system with the American one (e.g. self-reliance versus group solidarity, a future oriented versus a past oriented mentality), the process of cultural awareness is enhanced. Thus the cultural awareness achieved is both intracultural and intercultural.

Literary quotes: stereotypes and perceptions

Using literary texts is a well recognized approach to teaching cross-cultural communication. Literary texts are important cultural artefacts in foreign language learning, while literature is concerned with identity and self-awareness (Fenner, 2001: 13, 19).

The technique which is presented here relies on the intensive reading of poems and selected fragments of prose. At the beginning of the session using literary texts (or the first time when this technique is used during a longer course) students are presented with literary fragments related to national and racial stereotypes. Fragments of Agate Christie's novels (e.g. *Nemesis* or *Sleeping Murder. Miss Marple's Last Case*) may be used, taking advantage of the writer's ironic attitude to British ethnocentrism. Another useful fragment here may be an episode from Herman Melville's novel *Moby Dick*, in which the protagonist, Ishmael, first meets Queequeg, a native of an imaginary Kokovoko, somewhere "far away to the West and South. It is not down in any map; true places never are." (Melville, 1994: 70). In the course of the novel Queequeg becomes Ishmael's best friend, and also shows himself as the person aboard the *Pequod* who has more courage and integrity than any other crew member. At first, however, Ishmael is simply scared of him. The scene of the meeting between Ishmael and Queequeg in the Spouter-Inn shows excellently, and with a good deal of irony, Ishmael's original fear of and prejudice towards the person of another race and culture, which he gradually overcomes, realizing Queequeg's qualities, and concluding "he has just as much reason to fear me, as I have to be afraid of him. Better sleep with a sober cannibal than a drunken Christian" (Melville, 1994: 43).

There are also excellent poems to be used as literary representations of intercultural communication, e.g. Rudyard Kipling's "We and They" or the poem "Sure you can ask me personal questions" by the contemporary Native American poet Diane Burns. The value of poetry and poetic language in intercultural teaching is very high.

> Poetic language has a 'divided reference' to a real world as well as a fictional world because literary texts are experiments with thought: a dialectic between reality and fantasy. Through reading texts we gain an indirect understanding of the world, and, according to Ricoeur, this is a characteristic of poetic language. [According to Nicolaysen] reflections on a text allow the reader to turn interpretations upon him/herself and will consequently result in enhanced understanding and self-awareness. (Fenner, 2001: 19)

In the approach to the literary text presented here a poem (number 80) by Emily Dickinson is used as a transition to the second phase of the activities exploring literary texts, in which students are given quotations with a word taken out. The gap stands for the name of a country, a nationality or the name of the place. The students are shown the version with one word taken out and are told that the word refers to a nationality/culture. Their task is to figure out which nationality.

> Our lives are ....
> So still – so Cool
> Till some odd afternoon
> The Alps neglect their Curtain
> And we look farther on!
> *Italy* stands the other side!
> While like a guard between –
> The solemn Alps –
> The siren Alps
> Forever intervene!
>
> (Dickinson, 1990: 26)

The missing word is "Swiss" and there are students who can deduce it, using their knowledge of geography as well as the stereotype which the poem explores – the Swiss as cold and unemotional, while the Italians as the ones who are full of passion. And it is the reflection upon national stereotypes which is the main goal of this activity.

There are many samples of fragments of novels in which a similar technique can be applied. Since the task is done as a guessing game, students' mental processes are activated.

Particularly thought-provoking to Polish students are examples when literary fragments refer to Poles or Poland. An example may be given from the novel *Lady Oracle* by the Canadian author Margaret Atwood. The fragment presented to the students contains the following sentences with gaps, in the novel referring to a character whose name is Paul – of Polish nationality, as the students eventually learn.

> "On Monday he had to work at the bank, but in the evening he took me to dinner at a club for .... expatriates, which was full of one-eyed Generals and other .... Counts." (Atwood, 1982: 148)
>
> "He was compulsive about time, he had to leave the house at precisely eight-fifteen, and before that he spent ten minutes by the clock polishing his shoes and brushing his suit." (Atwood, 1982: 152)
>
> "Anyone from across the Atlantic ocean was a kind of savage to him, and even the English were questionable, they were too far west."
>
> "Then there were his views on the war. He seemed to think that the Jews were in some obscure way responsible for it, and thus for the loss of his family chateau."

> "For Paul had an end-of th-world fatalism: civilization for him had either already collapsed or was about to. He thought there would be another war, in fact he hoped there would; not that he thought it would solve or improve anything, but so that he himself might fight in it and distinguish himself by acts of bravery." (Atwood, 1982: 158)

The students' first likely guesses are Russian or German, but once they discover (or are told) that Paul is Polish, the fragments reveal several characteristics attributed to Polish culture: predilection to class distinctions, punctuality and cleanliness, the sense of superiority of old Polish culture over any other, and particularly North Americans, who are assumed to have no culture ("kind of savage"), anti-semitism, fatalism, the assumption that true glory comes from a death on the battlefield. Fatalism and glorious death in a battle reflect the deeply-rooted Polish sense that it is better to be a dead hero than a live contributor to the common good of the society. Aleksander Kamiński, discussing, in 1942, virtues and vices of Poles, enlisted as one of the vices the characteristic that "For Poles it is easier to die than to live for their country" (Mikulowski-Pomorski, 2006: 280).

The quoted fragments from Margaret Atwood's novel serve as an excellent springboard for intracultural dialogue. Students would have their own opinions, not always agreeing with the stereotype presented in Atwood's fiction, but the dialogue with the perception of own culture is inevitable. Even if the discussion is limited, because it might be linguistically too demanding for the students to discuss the issues raised by Atwood's text, the reflection is inevitable and the internal intracultural dialogue takes place within the student's mind. Whether silent or outspoken, each student becomes a participant in the dialogue.

Conclusion: relating to one's own culture

In conclusion it ought to be said that intracultural dialogue which takes place during intercultural activities is important for several reasons. There are obvious benefits of better understanding of one's own culture and its characteristic behavior patterns and emotional reactions. The improved understanding of one's own "software of the mind", to use Geert Hofstede's famous phrase, is essential in becoming a successful intercultural communicator.

Another benefit of the intracultural dialogue in the language classroom cannot be ignored – in practical experience it is our own culture that we are most often asked about and have to explain in contacts with people of other cultures. When surrounded by foreigners, whether abroad or in one's own country, we are perceived as experts in our own culture. Traditional ways of teaching culture, where students would be taught about the British "five o'clock tea" or what the notion "stiff upper lip" might refer to doubtless have their benefits, as they help the learner to function abroad. However, there is a greater likelihood of the Polish users of English as a foreign language being asked to explain the cultural tradition behind the Polish cabbage stew "bigos", or the Polish avoidance of eye contact and smile in contacts with strangers (probably stemming from a historically conditioned mistrust of strangers). As Ryszard Kapuściński (2006: 14) claimed when discussing Herodot, to understand yourself better, you have to learn about the Others, because They are the mirror in which we see ourselves. Through looking at the Other we may better understand our own culture, behavior and emotions, and only then can we try to explain ourselves to the Other.

Bibliography

Aleksandrowicz-Pędich, L., 2005, *Międzykulturowość na lekcjach języków obcych*, Białystok: Wydawnictwo Uniwersytetu w Białymstoku.

Atwood, M., 1982, *Lady Oracle*, London: Virago Press.

Bandura, E., 2007, *Nauczyciel jako mediator kulturowy*, Kraków: Tertium.

Birch, D., T. Schirato, S. Srivastava, 2001, *Asia: Cultural Politics in the Global Age*, St. Leonards, N.S.W.: Allen & Unwin. Accessed through <www.questia.com> (5 May 2007).

Clark, D.N., 2000, *Culture and Customs of Korea*, Westport, CT: Greenwood Press. Accessed through <www.questia.com> (5 May 2007).

Dickinson, E., 1990, *100 wierszy*, Kraków: Wydawnictwo Arka.

Fenner, A.B., 2001, *Cultural awareness and language awareness based on dialogic interaction with texts in foreign language learning*, Graz: European Centre for Modern Languages.

Huntington, S.P., 2002, *The Clash of Civilizations and the Remaking of the Word Order*, London: The Free Press.

Kapuściński, R., 2006, *Ten Inny*, Kraków: Znak.

Komorowska, H., 2006, "Intercultural competence in ELT syllabus and materials design", *Scripta Neophilologica Posnaniensia*, Vol. VIII, 59–81.

Maule, D., *Focus on Britain*. British Studies Web Pages. Accessed through <http: //elt. britcoun. org. pl / elt / v_scots.htm> (27 October 2007).

Melville, H., 1994, *Moby Dick*, London: Penguin Books.

Mikulowski-Pomorski, J., 2006, *Jak narody porozumiewają się ze sobą w komunikacji międzykulturowej i komunikowaniu medialnym*, Kraków: Wydawnictwo Universitas.

Shipler, D.K., 2002, *Arab and Jew. Wounded Spirits in a Promised Land*, London: Penguin Books.

Storti, C., (no date), *Culture Matters. The Peace Corps Cross-Cultural Workbook*, Washington: Peace Corps.

Swiderski, R.M., 1993, *Teaching Language, Learning Culture*, Westport, CT: Bergin & Garvey. Accessed through <www.questia.com> (5 May 2007).

Train, A., 1931, *Puritan's Progress: An Informal Account of Certain Puritans & Their Descendants from the American Revolution to the Present Time, Their Manners & Customs, Their Virtues & Vices. Together with Some Possibly Forgotten Episodes in the Development of American Social & Economic Life during the Last One Hundred & Fifty Year*, New York: Charles Scribner's Sons. Accessed through <www.questia.com> (30 April 2007).

Zawadzka, E., 2004, *Nauczyciele języków obcych w dobie przemian*, Kraków: Impuls.

DISCUSSION

Anna Niżegorodcew
Uniwersytet Jagielloński
Kraków

What culture and whose culture should we teach?

In L. Aleksandrowicz-Pędich's paper I find both approaches to teaching culture I have practised for years: an intercultural approach focusing on the target culture and an intracultural approach directing the students' attention towards our own culture. And the dilemmas involved in teaching about the Others through the mirror of ourselves in their eyes.

In fact, whenever I advertised a new course as a "cultural" course (usually teaching English combined with teaching culture), students believed that they would be studying some interesting aspects of the British or American culture (historical events and/or interesting people and places). My explanation during the first class with a new group of students that I would like to compare some aspects of the target and our own culture on the level of everyday life made them somehow less enthusiastic about the new course. They may not have been aware of the differences between their own and the target culture(s) on that ordinary level, and "culture" seemed to them to be the realm of the Unusual and the Sublime.

I remember a very successful "cultural" workshop for English teachers combined with a course developing their English language skills. The course had a rather cryptic name *Regional education in cross-curricular activities.* Since the English language school which conducted the course won a grant from the Małopolska region to make teachers more aware of its heritage and riches, the projects that were implemented in the workshop were entirely focused on various aspects of the region. Natural addressees of what the teachers found out about the Małopolska region were English speaking visitors. Consequently, not only the cultural tradition behind *bigos* was explained but also historical places and traditions were translated into English in a very concrete and practical way, e.g. some teachers prepared a guided tour for a group of English speaking visitors around the famous pilgrimage places at Kalwaria Zebrzydowska.

Liljana Skopinskaja
Tallinn University
Estonia

An intracultural approach to building intercultural communication skills: The description of a case study

The current article elaborates on a very vital aspect of foreign language instruction, namely preparing students for real-life encounters with the members of cultures other than their own. Although teaching intercultural awareness in a FL classroom is, as many studies have proved, of crucial importance, it is still often downplayed, at least at secondary school level, in the actual teaching due to the restrictions of a tight curriculum, unsuitable coursebooks, or plain unwillingness on the teachers' side. Thus the attempt to call attention to intercultural learning through intracultural awareness-raising ought to be seen as especially commendable.

To ensure training in intercultural awaress, teachers, course designers, and materials writers need to take into consideration at least two things: firstly, an organizational matrix to ensure that full coverage of socio-cultural conventions, beliefs, values, attitudes and behaviour patterns of one's own as well as foreign cultures, is incorporated in the course design; and secondly, a series of practical classroom activities which encourages a process of inter- and intracultural awareness-raising among FL learners. Although Aleksandrowicz-Pędich does not offer any conceptual framework for intercultural training, the titles of the activities presented in the article could constitute an organizational matrix in their own right, such as recognizing cultural images, examining cultural behaviour patterns, exploring values and attitudes, analysing stereotypes and cultural perceptions in literary works. Some of the activities offered are excellent. I particularly liked "Seven ways to annoy the Scots/Poles", which encourages the discussion of mutual representations of students' own stereotypes and those of other nationalities. The activities provided are mostly from Poland, but the points made can extend to any culture.

In sum, instructional materials should involve both local and international contexts so as to enable FL learners to become successful intercultural individuals.

Dorota Owczarek
Kolegium Języków Obcych
Uniwersytet im. Adama Mickiewicza
Poznań

How strange!

In my work with students during *British Life and Institution course* while discussing cultural aspects of life in Britain I encourage my students to present their opinion on what they see and hear in the documentaries that serve to illustrate a chosen aspect of culture. Their responses of the kind *how weird* or *it's funny* , in my opinion, clearly point to the cognitive processes that take place in students' minds that can be described as intercultural dialogue.

By referring to their native culture students find, at a first glance, another culture incomprehensible to some extent or simply different. This is only possible by activating their schemata which were developed in the process of socialization in their native culture and juxtaposing them with the cultural patterns they observe in the material presented to them during a lesson.

In order to help them understand the source of their reaction there occurs the need to explain to them how their own culture equips them with cultural patterns that lead to such statements. The process of analyzing their own culture begins, which L. Pędich in her article calls intracultural dialogue. The stages of a lesson during which both intercultural and intracultural dialogue is carried out include:

- immersion in a foreign culture via a video recording;
- reaction to the material presented;
- clarification of reaction on the basis of intercultural and intracultural dialogue.

The list of topics which serve the purpose of developing intercultural competence is, in fact, endless. L. Pędich has chosen the following ones: visiting a house, taking off shoes, kissing in public, eye-contact, nation's self-image, values (fate and destiny), stereotypes and perceptions of the other as presented in literature. The activities on which I based my observations focused on comparison of religious practices in Poland and Ireland. Students' opinions juxtaposed with the opinions presented in British Press on the freedom of an individual in reference to subcultures and the Public Order Bill introduced in Britain in 1994.

By going deep into one's own culture, it is possible to explain why our perception and description of another culture can be confined to words like: *funny*, *weird* or *strange*. It is only intracultural dialogue that may give light to the origins of such comments. If we take a closer look at our own culture, we will see how similar we are in human terms and how different in terms of our daily practices or values. I think there is no truer saying than the one Pędich gives at the end of her article: "Through looking at the Other we may better understand our own culture, behavior and emotions, and only then can we try to explain ourselves to the Other". This, in my opinion, puts in a nutshell the main message of intercultural training and specifies the goal for those who believe in educating "critical citizens for an intercultural world", the term coined by Guilherme, and which encourages us to approach critically both our own culture and the culture of the Other.

Bibliography

Guilherme, M., 2002, *Critical Citizens for an Intercultural World*, Clevedon Hall: Multilingual Matters.

Dorota Owczarek
Kolegium Języków Obcych
Uniwersytet im. Adama Mickiewicza
Poznań

The philosophical foundations for developing Intercultural Communicative Competence: The role of dialogue

The philosophical foundations lying at the base of intercultural communication and education reject the idea of instrumental reason and look for inspiration in Critical Theory or Gadamer's hermeneutics. The aim of this paper is to show how the idea of dialogue as developed by Bakhtin fills in the void uncovered by the afore mentioned philosophies and how problems unresolved by them can be explained on the basis of some concepts (especially the idea of dialogue, heteroglossia and border) introduced into language philosophy by Bakhtin.

The role of education nowadays is not focused on one particular aspect of human development but more on the holistic idea of educating the whole man. Therefore, philosophical foundations, such as Critical Theory or Gadamer's hermeneutics, standing behind Intercultural Communicative Competence (ICC) are extended over the field of general pedagogy of man rather than over a narrow stretch of language education. Since the aim of language education is the wellbeing of the whole person and influencing her/his worldviews and attitudes towards others, it is also perceived as the one that contributes to the language pedagogy. Philosophies in question offer new solutions to these educational needs by focusing on the development of critical thinking as in Critical Theory or on Bildung as in Gadamer's hermeneutics. Reflexivity or rejection of a biased attitude in one's attempt to reach understanding are the assets of critical thinking, and they were adopted for the purpose of developing ICC. Gadamer's hermeneutics with its idea of the fusion of horizons seems to correspond to the idea of the third place in ICC and it also suggests looking at the development of ICC as the holistic process. Thus, language education creates the possibility to examine and reflex on the nature of relations with others and discover and shape one's identity. This can be achieved via communication with the other or with the text (literary text included and given its priority especially for the purpose of aesthetic education and also for the richness of its choice). Despite the unquestionable merits of these philosophies for language pedagogy in paying attention to the role of critical thinking in intercultural communication and in the perception of the integral education of a person, it seems however that the idea of dialogue as developed by Bakhtin deserves more prominence and can help overcome drawbacks of the mentioned philosophies. Before pinpointing how Bakhtinian concepts can enhance the idea of ICC, let us look in more detail at the connections between ICC and Critical Theory and Gadamer's hermeneutics.

ICC is the competence needed for a successful intercultural interaction. It is composed of skills, attitudes towards foreign cultures, mediation skills and knowledge of a foreign culture. The ultimate goal in the development of ICC is critical cultural awareness, which Byram (1997: 53) defines in the following way: "An ability to evaluate critically and on the basis of explicit criteria perspectives, practices and products in one's own and other cultures and countries." Byram adds (1997: 54) that the important point is that "the intercultural speaker brings to the experiences of their own and other cultures a rational and explicit standpoint from which to evaluate." Byram argues that "appropriately structured experience of and reflection on otherness can develop levels of understanding and moral judgement" (Byram, 1997: 54). In short, critical cultural awareness means approaching foreign cultures critically.

As it is presented in depth by Guilherme in her book *Critical Citizens for an Intercultural World* (2002) the idea of critical cultural awareness is developed on the basis of Critical Theory, which constitutes the basic philosophical foundation for bringing into focus the concept of understanding and how it is achieved as well as the ability to judge. Based on her readings of Horkheimer, Adorno and Habermas, Guilherme gives the main tenets of Critical Theory and their relevance for ICC. First, critical reason is developed through social interactions (as opposed to the view of instrumental reason). According to Critical Theory "the individual does not exist independently from society, individual consciousness is interwoven with social processes and knowledge is socially produced (Guilherme, 2002: 69). Second, unlike the instrumental reason, critical reason is capable of self-reflection. Critical Theory is deeply rooted in the social political and therefore the critical thinking is oriented towards emancipation, which means "the power of reflection" (Guilherme, 2002: 68). Third, Critical Theory also redefines the relation between the subject and the object, namely as opposed to the previously cherished view that the subject is the person that strives to understand and get to know the object, Critical Theory favors the concept of intersubjective reason. The object is replaced by another subject, and what is more the subject is perceived as a social subject entangled in the social relations of the world around. In other words it is positioned in culture and history.

According to Guilherme Habermas' theory is also worth considering when dealing with intercultural communication because of the fact that his Theory of Communicative Action is built on the practice placed in social settings and aimed at reaching understanding (Guilherme, 2002: 73). As she explains through the so called illocutionary acts the reader aims for mutual understanding and consensus. She finds Habermas' model the one that "allows for culturally more open societies" and "since the goal of communicative action is to reach an understanding and to co-ordinate action, it is oriented towards establishing norms which, theoretically, reflect reciprocal expectations, and are rationally and intersubjectively justified and agreed upon" (Guilherme, 2002: 75). According to Guilherme Habermas' Theory of Comunicative Action and Critical Theory both underline the role of reflexive thinking in communication and thus overcome ideology that otherwise might foreshadow understanding (Guilherme, 2002: 80–81).

There are seemingly divergent points between the views presented by Habermas and Bakhtin. The indisputable similarity lies in the move they both show towards intersubjective orientation in a communicative event. Therefore, both Habermas and Bakhtin pave the way for a pedagogy of dialogue, which aims at empowering students to speak their own voice in interactions with their teacher. For both philosophers the relationship between subjects in communication is of dialogical position in which the subjects negotiate their self-representations and identity (Guilherme, 2002: 70). However, this is also where their ideas diverge. Habermas, according to Guilherme, advocates the capacity to establish interpersonal relations and emphasizes mutual understanding to be reached by the subjects in interaction. This understanding is to occur within two dimensions: the moral dimension and the ethical dimension. "These dimensions are complementary and provide both for unity and plurality, for transcendence and immanence in discourse. [...] Within the moral dimension the individual appeals to a universal discourse that exceeds the boundaries of a limited group" (Guilherme, 2002: 71). This idea of a universal dimension as well as the existence of universal meanings puts Habermas and his ideas miles apart from Bakhtin's. Although Guilherme finds it important in her view on educating critical citizens for an intercultural world, a moral/universal dimension is far too broad in my understanding to be realized in a subject-subject model of interaction. This is the empty space that can be filled with Bakhtin's idea of dialogue relying on personal experience of participants of a dialogue and their mutual responsiveness. "Understanding is always dialogic to some degree" Bakhtin (2004: 111). Hence, instead of aiming at some universal dimension the emphasis should be put on the dialogic relations leading to understanding.

Other limitations of Habermas' model lie in his universal norms as preconditions of understanding and the role of power relations in communication. As Guilherme describes it, in Habermas' model both participants must be able to understand what is said to each of them, the statement has to be considered true by both parties and both interlocutors have to believe each other to be truthful (Guilherme, 2002: 75–76). These norms have to be universally recognized, and the unifying ground for participants in a communicative act is the function of rationality. Another drawback discussed by Guilherme is Habermas' disregard for the role of power relations and attribution of the same weight of interests to parties involved in communication. She admits that Habermas' theory is ethnocentric and Eurocentric. Despite those drawbacks Guilherme, whose point is that critical citizens of an intercultural world should be educated so as to develop "the potential of reason for the purpose of democratic emancipation" and strive towards democratic unitary thinking (Guilherme, 2002: 81), still believes that Habermas' theory is useful as a philosophical foundation for communication across cultures in the way it"provides the tools for the dialogic construction of the space for intercultural communication" and finding common ground that transcends the horizon of the lifeworld (Guilherme, 2002: 79). It is believed that all those drawbacks presented here can be overcome by incorporating Bakhtinian idea of dialogue into the philosophical foundations for developing ICC.

The second philosophy that interests us here is Gadamer's hermeneutics and his idea of horizons. By Guilherme Gadamer is only mentioned in passing. Guilherme explains that "for Gadamer horizon is not necessarily rigid or limiting, something we cannot surpass, but a line from where we can see what lies beyond and which also moves with us." According to Gadamer "the process of achieving understanding means a fusion of horizons" (Guilherme, 2002: 78). "Reaching an understanding in conversation presupposes that both partners are ready for it and are trying to recognize the full value of what is alien and opposed to them" (Gadamer, 1970: 348 after Guilherme, 2002: 78). Although Gadamer doubts the possibility of reaching agreement, like Habermas he also sheds off positivistic views of communication and positions the subject within his own and other's prejudices and perspectives. The man brings into a communicative act prejudices and historicity and can move beyond them (Guilherme, 2002: 78).

Gadamer's ideas for the purpose of intercultural communication have been developed by Roy and Starosta. In the process of understanding man all presumptions and biases should be bracketed and qualified so as to be able to understand the perspective of the other and compare it to one's own (Roy and Starosta, 2001: 9). Since language plays a central part in understanding, Gadamer proposes a dialogic model that is similar to Socratic one in the sense that the relations are dialogic. He develops his model on the basis of dialogic relations between the text and the reader. Gadamer believes that truth can emerge only from the genuine dialogue between them. In this model the text is not treated as the object but as the subject. Understanding is reached through "transcending to a higher universality that overcomes not only one's own particularity, but that of other's as well" (Roy and Starosta, 2001: 10). Such understanding depends on one's awareness of different modes of self and world description and the ability to discriminate, which is called by Gadamer Buildung. Buildung incorporates notions of tact, taste and judgment (Roy and Starosta, 2001: 10). Gadamer's hermeneutics is useful for intercultural communication in the sense that it advocates "context-sensitive approaches, i.e. approaches cognizant and appreciative of context and history, which means that understanding stems from tradition and texts, experiences and actions need be understood and interpreted in a historical context. [...] Actions and expressions of individuals can properly be understood by reference to their cultural context" (Roy and Starosta, 2001: 11–12). Gadamer, as Roy and Starosta see it, asks communicators to be aware of the existence of prejudice and use it productively, be open, which means to reveal their prejudices and to question them by prejudices of the other (Roy and Starosta, 2001: 13). What also can be derived from Gadamer and is of high value for intercultural understanding is the fact that going through a self-forming process (Building) one develops one's sensitivity and character, but before one starts to appreciate other cultures he/she needs "to immerse in their own culture and make sense of their own people and develop a capacity for judgment and taste" (Roy and Starosta, 2001: 16). "In intercultural communication studies there should be linkages between communication, identity, power and knowledge across cultures" (Roy and Starosta, 2001: 13). Those who study culture and get engaged in this through studying literary texts should stress dialogic relations on which this study is based and remember about differences that run through cultures that need be compared (Roy and Starosta, 2001: 14).

Habermas called for a universality of values in intercultural communication, Gadamer thinks intercultural communication research should derive from a moral base (Roy and Starosta, 2001: 13). In other words they both assume a kind of universal platform for intercultural contacts. In Gadamer's hermeneutics a competent intercultural researcher moves from immediacy and particularity towards universality. Buildung aids such a person to hold a universal point of view, stay open and committed to "the fundamental unity of all human beings" (Roy and Starosta, 2001: 16). This universal moral ground brings Gadamer closer to Habermas. They both aim at some universal features of intercultural discourse. According to Gadamer's hermeneutics in studying cultures the important thing is to put aside the a priori cultural differences and co-create knowledge in a way that does not privilege one position over another (Roy and Starosta, 2001: 14–15). This is where Gadamer and Bakhtin largely converge, i. e. both parties should speak their own voice in dialogic relations. In the likewise manner Habermas' idea of communication relies on the diversity of voices (Guilherme, 2002: 81). However, Godich (2002) makes an important remark on the seeming similarities between Gadamer and Bakhtin.

> The dialogic is a sociotheoretical notion through which a view of postmodern society is articulated as a society organized around central conflict of its cultural orientation....Nor is Bakhtin's dialogic to be confused with a Gadamerian conversation in which one loses oneself or in which there occurs a fusion of horizons. The central notion of dialogic is agonistic. It is a refusal of symbiosis and a rejection of the undifferentiated; it is meant to allow the conflictual definitions of differences as constitutive elements of a postrevolutionary and postmodern society. It would establish the rule of Altruity. (Godich, 2003: 13)

In other words, for Gadamer understanding means the fusion of horizons and for Habermas some kind of universality. For Bakhtin, however, it is clear that such option does not exist. The essence of communication lies in the very idea of dialogue where two subjects meet only to discover their opposing views and realize different voices they speak. Such an encounter does not bring them closer to understanding each other but only to become more aware of their own opinions and how they might be perceived by the other. The dialogic relations enable the move towards the other, but then again withdrawal to one's own position enlightened by the new perspective given by the other. The dialogic relations are of conflictual nature as Godich (2003) notices, and the option that Bakhtin allows for in such relations is not the common moral base but the concern for the needs and feelings of the other, which is not tantamount to empathy, which Bakhtin clearly rejects in his writing. This concern means the allowance for everyone to speak their own voice that is grounded in one's social and historical experience.

Bakhtin in discussing understanding directs our attention to the context, here and now and to the idea of dialogue itself. Therefore, in the light of Bakhtin's arguments it might be said that intercultural contacts create a great opportunity to discover one's own culture and one's own position, thus leading to a new perspective on oneself. The discussions of ICC focus on critical cultural awareness as the main objective of developing ICC in the process of becoming critical citizens of an intercultural world. The point is that the weight of the problem should be moved to the role of dialogue as the main prerequisite of intercultural relations. Only true dialogic relations allow people to become responsible and worthy citizens who can speak their own voice and recognize the voices of the other. Hence, it is proposed that dialogic pedagogy together with language education should promote the concept of cultural dialogue that would highlight the following objectives:

- to be aware of my own voice;
- to be aware of the voices of others;
- to be aware that the dialogue helps to look at my point of view from a new perspective;
- to be able to change my position or keep it (to be flexible);
- to withdraw from my position or come back if I wish so.

This emphasis on the role of the speakers' voices in a dialogue as well as their complexity brings us directly to the concept of heteroglossia. Heteroglossia is "a perception of language ideologically saturated and stratified" (Morris, 1994: 15). Without such awareness of language which is filled with ideologies that limit the perception of the world a true dialogue cannot happen. The understanding that in a dialogue speakers actually confront their ideologies might help participants of the dialogue realize why their points of view contrast and clash so much.

Now let us look at the idea of borderline and what it brings to the concept of dialogue. The idea of borderline is where the parties of a dialogue meet. Though not always easily noticed, it constitutes the background against which words from an utterance of one party of a dialogue are contrasted with the words from the other party. This borderline is the abstract place where the meanings of the words speakers use as well as their viewpoints meet. This means that actually no word in a dialogue can be defined without its reference to the words already used in an utterance. Even more, words used in an utterance very often go beyond the present context of an utterance and reach to the life experience of the speaker. Sometimes words are colored by parody or irony (Bakhtin, 1984 cited in Morris, 1994: 107–108). Then, the borderline, always present in dialogic relations, may be difficult to point at.

It is believed that if the idea of dialogue in intercultural relations be given a more prominent position, the parties involved in such relations will feel more at ease in expressing themselves and taking into account the position of other parties . "Truth is not born nor is it to be found inside the head of an individual person, it is born between people collectively searching for truth, in the process of their dialogic interaction" (Bakhtin, 1984: 110 after Mey, 1999: 235). It seems that in the publications presented so far the ultimate goal of ICC was to educate critical citizens for an intercultural world (Guilherme, Byram and Risager). These models focused on the final product in the form of a citizen belonging to the globalized world. The author of this article believes that the weight of attention should shift to the process of becoming such citizen. By this it is meant that the role of dialogue should be stressed. This would position the whole idea of developing ICC in a broad spectrum of dialogic pedagogy and would give it a more active dimension. In other words, the role of education would be in spurring students to action rather than to absorbing skills and knowledge. It is also believed that the Bakhtinian idea of dialogue may successfully complement Critical Theory and Gadamer's hermeneutics as a philosophical foundation for developing ICC.

Bibliography

Bakhtin, M., 1984, *Problems of Dostoevsky's Poetics*, 1963, transl. C. Emerson, Minneapolis, Minn.: Minnesota Press.

Bakhtin, M., 2004, *Speech Genres and Other Late Essays*, Austin: University of Texas Press.

Byram, M., 1997, *Teaching and Assessing Intercultural Communicative Competence*, Clevedon: Multilingual Matters.

Gadamer, H.G., 1970, *Truth and Method*, London: Sheed and Ward.

Godich, W., 2003, "Correcting Kant: Bakhtin and Intercultural Interactions", [in:] M. Gardiner, ed., *Mikhail Bakhtin*, London: Sage Publ.

Guilherme, M., 2002, *Critical Citizens for an Intercultural World*, Clevedon: Multilingual Matters.

Mey, J.L., 1999, *When Voices Clash. A Study in Literary Pragmatics*, Berlin, New York: Mouton de Gruyter.

Morris, P., ed., 1994, *The Bakhtin Reader: Selected Writings of Bakhtin, Medvedev, Voloshinov*, London: Arnold.

Roy, A., W.J. Starosta, 2001, "Hans-Georg Gadamer, Language, and Intercultural Communication", *Language and Intercultural Communication*, Vol. 1, 6–20.

DISCUSSION

Liljana Skopinskaja
Tallinn University
Estonia

The commitment to theory: Searching for the theoretical foundations of intercultural communicative competence

The current article discusses, and does it most convincingly, the philosophical foundations underlying the development of intercultural communicative competence (ICC). ICC has become a catchword for our times, and any publication in this field is therefore welcome as a tool for looking analytically and critically at this concept.

From the outset, the author displays erudition in background studies, providing at every step, useful and relevant information. The focus of the discussion – complementation of Gadamer's hermeneutics with Bakhtinian idea of dialogue with the view of providing a philosophical foundation for ICC – is novel, since the studies of intercultural communication in Europe have hitherto been linked to areas such as anthropological sociolinguistics, pragmatics and discourse analysis rather than to humanistic disciplines like hermeneutics, semiotics or postmodernism. The philosophical terms analysed – dialogue, fusion of horizons, heteroglossia, borderline – are, however, useful as far as intecultural awareness is concerned because the latter involves the shifting of identities where we are in the other, and the other is in us. In other words, while learning a foreign language, the student brings his or her own culture into the communication process, whether it is in reading a foreign text or holding a conversation. Interpreting the meaning of the foreign text or the interlocutor's message is also interpreting one's own self. Likewise, in acquiring knowledge about the target language culture, the learner not only observes the similarities and differences between the two cultures, his own and the foreign one, but also analyses them from the viewpoint of the other, thus trying to establish a relationship between his own and other systems.

The ideas raised in this article are particularly relevant for incorporating literature into the FL instruction, since the student enters into a dialogue with the text and the foreign culture in the process of reading thus trying to produce meaning from the polyphony of that particular text.

Anna Niżegorodcew
Uniwersytet Jagielloński
Kraków

Some doubts about "spurring students to action"

I like a clear and confident voice of the author with which she presents Habermas's, Gadamer's and Bakhtin's philosophical ideas. For her it is Bakhtin whose philosophy of dialogue provides the best foundations for the development if intercultural communicative competence.

A clear description and clearly formulated preferences recall my own early fascination with philosophical thought. The author is a teacher educator. How fortunate are her trainees – I think. But she also writes that "the role of education would be in spurring students to action rather than to absorbing skills and knowledge". At this moment I ask myself – What action? An educational well-prepared action, like a school reform or an action research project? Or any revolutionary action which takes advantage of young people's enthusiasm in order to abolish old powers and replace them by the new ones?

We have had enough of it: *Liberty, Equality, Fraternity!* or *Proletarians of All Countries Unite!* Great words and villainous deeds. Why is it that Bakhtin's philosophy of dialogue seems to be another such slogan? Just like sociocultural theory of second language acquisition. Do contemporary American sociolinguists and SLA theorists realize that what was written in the Soviet Union by linguists, psychologists and philosophers could not be deprived of ideological pressures.

Even if quite a lot of what we hear now from American descendents of Vygotsky and Gal'perin is true, such claims as *thought is action*, are dangerously close to the most notorious slogan of my school days in the Polish People's Republic: *Byt kształtuje świadomość* (Reality shapes thinking). Such slogans are meaningless for my generation. They have been ridiculed to the extent which does not allow me to use them any more in any discourse except an ironical one.

It seems that Polish patronizing and ridiculing attitude towards the Russian language may be a consequence of the same process of overgeneralization of old traumas associated with the ideological impact of the language enforced upon the Poles. Indeed *thought is action* and words associated with negative actions are emotionally loaded with negative, or at best patronizing feelings.

Besides, Intercultural Communicative Competence may find its foundations in the philosophy of dialogue but the philosophy must be translated into classroom activities. Otherwise teachers will pass exams in dialogic philosophy but in class they will focus on knowledge and skills.

Lucyna Aleksandrowicz-Pędich
Szkoła Wyższa Psychologii Społecznej
Warszawa

The importance of theoretical foundations for successful intercultural communication

It seems doubtless that developing intercultural communicative competence is not only a practical activity involving accurately selected tasks, but an educational endeavor requiring solid theoretical basis. Introducing the philosophical background to the study of ICC stresses the notion that ICC is not only a "know-how" indicating proper behavior rituals, but most of all awareness of the implications of different modes of thinking and the impact of ideological standings of the partners in a communication process, leading to its success or failure.

We may wonder whether a competent intercultural mediator does exist as the final product of educational efforts – perhaps being competent is a process that expands over each meeting with the Other, assuming a component of novelty in each encounter. Becoming involved in the process of intercultural communication one should be strongly aware of, on the one hand, the option of achieving Gadamer's "fusion of horizons" as mentioned in Dorota Owczarek's article, but, on the other, of the prospect of retaining one's position, which is fixed by social and historical background, and only having it better illuminated through understanding the perspective of the Other. The second option stresses how much intercultural contacts affect intracultural perception and one's own identity. Intercultural dialogue may lead to the process of self-discovery, provided, however, that it takes place in the awareness of the composite and multi-dimensional nature of the process.

The introduction of Bakhtin to the field of intercultural competence is important not only for his ideas on dialogism, but for yet another reason – Bakhtin has made contributions to a great variety of intellectual fields. His thoughts are used by literary critics, linguists, anthropologists, philosophers. He moved on the borders of disciplines and his inspiration for scholars to come was highly interdisciplinary. Relating to various disciplines reflects also the nature of intercultural experiences. One cannot hope to achieve ICC without drawing upon a great diversity of fields of knowledge, while an understanding of intercultural experience may be explained by not just one, but various philosophical approaches.

Wojciech Majka
Uniwersytet Jagielloński
Kraków

Dasein's Temporal Horizon

Before providing my own extension to the ideas insinuated by the article I would like to look back to it for just a moment. Besides the central theme founded upon the Bakhtinian dialectics with the foreshadowing of the concept of *raznorechie* (heteroglossia), the article also hints at, perhaps a little unconsciously, other vast philosophical possibilities. For example, two of the problems that are touched upon refer to the Husserlian idea of *epoché* (a bracketing of the world) and the notion of the horizon, which is affixed to the idea of intentionality. However, for some reason the author does not think it necessary to refer to the basics of phenomenology.

The phenomenon of critical thinking that the article also develops goes back to the "midwifery" of Socratic and Platonic tradition. Let us not forget that it is really this idea that is developed in *Phaedrus*. Here Plato discusses the virtues of Theuth's gift of writing to Thamus by silhouetting writing against the breathing voice of the soul, i.e. speech. Plato observes that writing possesses only a representative mode of being and for this reason it is compared to painting that is incapable of speaking to the perceiver. The same applies to the written word which does not control the mind that seeks to interpret it. In speech, however, the speaker has control over the message and the medium of expression can be modulated and appropriated to the needs of the audience. What we are dealing here with is a situation of a dialogue based on the relation between that which represents (writing) and the mind of the perceiver. In short, this theory is really based on Plato's idea of *anamnesis*, where knowledge and understanding were said to be obtained by means of memory. Thus language automatically became the medium in the dialogue between the present self and its former incarnations, as Plato (or rather Pythagoras) would have it.

The status of language that is the material of any content transmission is addressed very interestingly by Heidegger. The author of *Sein und Zeit* believed that we are never in control of language or as he famously put it, it is not that we are in a position to speak language but rather it is language that speaks us. This understanding of language is really based on a much profounder concept of being and on Dasein's position in it.

Generally put, Dasein can be equalled with self-consciousness. A self awareness which is not an act of rational thinking like in *cogito ergo sum* where the act of thinking is self contemplative. Heidegger's self-consciousness is an emotionally practical connection with the world; with the decisions and choices that one has to make in practical life.

Dasein's being is based on the horizon of temporality. If time, or history is so important for the being of Dasein, as it predetermines or predestines its individual existence, then we in our analysis also have to take account of that very history; in other words, in hermeneutical analysis we have to try to understand not only the object but its historical context as well, since the meanings that we believe in are all historically predetermined. Henceforth, the now of my present experience is based on the past; in this way the present moment is always fleeting, in this way the consciousness of every present moment is already the consciousness of the past. Robert Frost poeticizes the theme in the following way:

Nature's first green is gold,
Her hardest hue to hold.
Her early leaf's a flower
But only so an hour.
Then leaf subsides to leaf.
So Eden sank to grief,
So dawn goes to day,
Nothing gold can stay.

As I have mentioned above to commit ourselves to a process of understanding we have to understand the tradition and history behind things, since if we do not then that history and tradition will bias our view of the object we are examining. For this very reason we should not avoid history but instead reconstruct it and discover the way that it determines our view of the world and the thing that we are examining. Doing this we will perform a Schopenhauerian reversification of individual perceptions to the contexts that furnished them. On the other hand, the reconstruction of the tradition for cultural understanding of being is very much reminiscent of the Pythagorean *anamnesis* that was later developed by Plato.

But time has yet another very important meaning for the being of Dasein. It seems that Dasein is thrown into a world that is not of its own choosing. In such a world, being is always a being-unto death and Dasein can never trespass the bounds of its finite existence. This finitude is what we have forgotten about when we think of our own being and the world that circumscribes us.

In order to escape the falsity and inauthenticity of our own existence we have to embrace death and engage in a dialogue with nothingness. Facing nothingness we are obliged to rethink what being means in the first place. This quest for the meaning of being is what is called fundamental ontology, an ontology that will allow us to look at being through the inherent structures of Dasein. The analysis of the inherent structures of Dasein shows that the horizon against which the being of any being can be understood is temporality. Thus existence is a constant dialogue between Dasein and its temporal horizon.

Joanna Rokita-Jaśkow
Akademia Pedagogiczna
Kraków

Parent-child dyads: Fostering or inhibiting second language learning?

It is a truism to say that a child learns to speak through verbal interaction with his/her parents. Therefore it can be said that language acquisition is the outcome of ongoing dialogue between the two parties.

This paper is going to focus on the forms of dialogue/interaction that lead to the development of communicative ability in a very young child in a second language. It is assumed that the role of the parent in creating a multifaceted and linguistically rich dialogue will be equally important in first and second language acquisition and learning. I will try to demonstrate when the form of dialogue, or more precisely the discourse strategies used within it, foster second language learning and when they inhibit it. (Following Krashen's (1981) distinction, here the term "learning" is preferred to the term "acquisition", as this refers to subjects learning L2 in an instructional setting).

The role of parent-child dyads in L1 acquisition

The assumption that language is acquired through verbal interaction between a child and his/her parents is maintained by the interactionist view of language acquisition (e.g. Newport, Gleitman and Gleitman, 1977; Tomasello, 1998). According to this position, language develops through the interplay of a child's cognitive abilities and the linguistic input that he/she receives as well as the things which he/she observes, touches or uses. This means the child acquires words for particular objects or actions when he/she hears them labeled, and hypothesizes about the rules of language when his/her interlocutors rephrase his/her speech.

Interactionists ascribe an important role to a child-directed speech, i.e. the language of adult interlocutors (usually a parent), which is modified and adjusted to the child's current level. This modification is vital as comprehension is a necessary condition for language to be acquired. As a result, most child-adult conversations focus on "here" and "now", i.e. on the actions currently happening and surrounding objects, for both an adult and a child. It is necessary for an adult to take note of what interests the child and then talk about it rather than make the child focus on the adult's area of interest. Therefore

joint attention is a key feature of successful dialogue which will generate input suitable for acquisition (Tomasello, 1998).

In establishing joint attention, parents usually follow the direction the child is looking in or react to a child pointing to an object or turning towards something. Also, adults generally follow the topics generated by the child; expanding and commenting on what was already conversationally present (Clark, 2003). Quite naturally, it is possible to establish joint attention in such activities as playing with toys, reading/looking through a book, eating a meal, changing a diaper and routine games (such as "peek-a-boo"), etc.

By asking children to take turns in a conversation, parents teach them how to actively participate. Initially, the child's contribution to a conversation is minimal and takes the form of touching a picture, vocalizing, looking at his/her interlocutor and smiling. Yet, these show that the child is actively involved in negotiating the meaning. As the child becomes more skilled at taking turns, he/she makes more relevant contributions by nodding or even by asking full clarification questions ("Did you mean X or Y?") and adults ask for more explicit expressions of the meanings intended (Clark, 2003).

Similar views about the role of verbal interaction in language development have been voiced by renowned psychologists, Lev Vygotsky and Jerome Bruner. Their observations and ideas have very much contributed to our understanding of how children acquire language. To describe the role of parents in the process, they both coined terms critical to their teaching. Vygotsky introduced the term: **Zone of Proximal Development** (ZPD), by which he meant the difference between current knowledge of the child and the knowledge which can be acquired under the supervision of others. The parent's role was to tune in to the child's ZPD by modeling the learning task (here language learning), dividing it into segments and highlighting key aspects to the child. As the child develops skills in this area, less parental help is given. Multiple repetitions of the same task finally make it automatic. The child's role in this kind of learning is that of an apprentice learning from the more knowledgeable master (Schaffer, 2006).

Bruner, in turn, introduced the term "**scaffolding**" to describe how parents help a child in solving a problem, how they adjust the extent and the type of help to the child's abilities. In the case of a language learning task, they modify their speech by gradually involving their children in the conversation until they completely take the lead. The kinds of strategies that they use to solve tasks are, e.g. drawing the child's attention to the task, simplifying the task by breaking it down into smaller steps, reminding the child of the goal of the activity, pointing out an important activity and showing the child other ways of doing it, controlling the child's frustration, demonstration of an idealized version of the task and praising the child. These strategies can be equally applied both to nonverbal tasks (such as jigsaw puzzles) and verbal tasks (e.g. joint storytelling based on a book) (Schaffer, 2006).

To summarize, the findings of both psychologists were similar and both recognized the role of social interaction with adult interlocutors in the development of speech, among other learning tasks.

The role of parent-child dyads in L2 acquisition

The interactionist theory has also had an impact on second language acquisition. Researchers working in this field, e.g. Michael Long (1983), Teresa Pica (1987), Susan Gass (1997), have developed Krashen's innatist theory of language acquisition, which roughly states that in order for a language to be acquired, language input has to be comprehensible. Therefore they focused on the issue how to make the input comprehensible.

As a model they took the interactional modifications that native speakers use when they talk to non-native speakers. These interactional modifications include both non--linguistic simplifications, such as slower speech rate, gestures, pointing to an object, and linguistic ones, such as comprehension checks, clarifications requests, repetition and paraphrasing.

Only the language input that is comprehensible can be subsequently taken in, that is assimilated and matched against the existent knowledge of the learner. Thus **intake** and **integration** constitute further stages of language development. This means that not all linguistic input is readily integrated but rather new information is compared with prior knowledge. This is the stage where generalizations are likely to occur and memory traces are formed. Thus the integration of new material with old can take two forms: development of the second language grammar or the storage of new information. The final stage is **output** which serves as a means of hypothesis testing, i.e. once a learner has created a hypothesis about a second language form, he/she should try to use it in some form of production. The feedback which he/she obtains as a result, will either modify or reinforce the information received initially. Therefore output serves as feedback into the intake (Swain, 1985).

Output plays an important role in forcing the learner to syntactically analyze the produced utterance. While it is not necessary to pay attention to the syntax of an utterance while listening to a message (a general understanding of key lexis and situational context will do), it is very important to follow the correct word order when producing a sentence. Swain (1985) referred to this ability as **comprehensible output** and defined it as pushing the learner "toward the delivery of a message that is not only conveyed, but that is conveyed precisely, coherently, and appropriately" (1985: 249). In other words, linguistic input can be regarded as acquired if it can manifest itself in correct and comprehensible output. For this reason it is indispensable that the learner not only shows comprehension (as in innatist position) but also attempts to produce language.

Such views of language acquisition have had an impact on language pedagogy. There has been a shift from prolonging the so called "silent period", on the grounds that it can denote incomprehension (cf. Gibbons, 1985), to forcing the learner to language production, as only language that is produced provides evidence of the acquisition process taking place.

Interestingly, a similar need to force the learner to L2 production was noticed by parents bringing up their children bilingually in situations when they noticed inadequate development in the minority language. The first notable example of that sort comes from Takahiro, a Japanese boy who came to the US at the age of 2;6 (Itoh and Hatch, 1978). He was enrolled in an American kindergarten with a view to acquiring English along with Japanese. However, despite favorable conditions, i.e. natural immersion in L2, Takahiro's L2 (English) development was very slow. After 3 months he was able only to repeat single words involuntarily after his adult interlocutors. This slow progress made the parents and researchers (Itoh and Hatch, 1978), who were the friends of the family, believe that the child had problems with understanding the language in his new environment. Therefore they decided to supply the child with more explicit instruction in L2. They adopted such discourse strategies as **call for repetition, giving picture reference**, **giving answer prompts**, and **request for clarification**. After only a month of such instruction the child entered the stage of spontaneous speech and was able to combine lexical items freely for communicative purposes. Apparently, in the beginning the child was shocked and stressed by the novelty of the situation. What he needed was some help from adults in clarifying the new language and adjusting it to his current level of ability. What proved useful for his speech development was the pressure to use the second language. Takahiro's example best illustrates how the comprehensible output feeds back into the linguistic input received.

Following Takahiro's case, there have been numerous studies into bilingual acquisition, either in a family or in a kindergarten setting, with a view to identifying discourse strategies which in a similar way help to promote the development of the minority language. The following strategies have additionally been found to be effective: **avoiding code-mixing** (Genesee, 1989; Juan-Garau and Perez-Vidal, 2001), **request for information, object labeling, stating intention, labeling action** (Cathcart-Strong, 1986), **using formulas and routines** (Kanagy, 1999).

In addition, when researching different types of interaction in a kindergarten setting, Damhuis (1992) found that the largest amount of comprehensible output, i.e. the largest number of correct utterances, was produced during formal instruction of L2. However, the majority of utterances constituted answers to the teacher's questions, which denotes learning rather than true communication. L2 child learners initiated most utterances during free play with native speaking (Dutch) children. This is also when they obtained most verbal and non-verbal feedback. However, the feedback obtained from native speaking children is often limited to answering the non-native children's questions. This, in turn, does not encourage non-native children to continue the conversation.

The second type of interaction which evoked a longer response from non-native children was activities in a small group with a teacher. In such a situation the teacher is able to devote more attention to each individual child and tune in to the child's current interests, e.g. by asking him/her about the toy he/she is playing with or joining the child in an activity such as drawing, looking through a book etc. In such activities the adult interlocutor (here the teacher) is able to maintain conversation, and thus provide more language input, by labeling objects, asking for information, commenting on the activities. It seems the joint attention of an adult and a child on the same topic generates more comprehensible output. The role of an adult interlocutor is very important as he/she can help the child learner by supporting his/her L2 production much more than another child. Damhuis (1992) concludes that in kindergarten settings when there are non-native speaking children more hours should be devoted to activities in which there is "one-to-one" or "one-to-a few" interaction, the adult interlocutor being in the centre. Such a solution, however, may not be very realistic or practical. Recognizing the role of an adult in generating comprehensible output, it seems that a family situation and a parent may constitute the best environment for the development of the second language by a child.

Forms of a dialogue in L2 instruction

Having identified successful discourse strategies in natural bilingualism, it seems only justifiable to transfer them to situations in which L2 is acquired via instruction, i.e. when the amount of available L2 input is severely limited, and particularly when language learners are very young children (below the age of 4), who are still in the process of acquiring their mother tongue. A similar parental role should be recognized here: the parent should be the provider of L2 input, and generator of the child's comprehensible output. Joint attention in activities such as play, reading stories, daily routines, etc. helps to create a multitude of topics for realistic conversations and providing varied L2 input.

A key question arises, however, if instructed child learners can acquire L2, provided one creates similar conditions, i.e. actively engages in verbal interactions with the child and uses similar discourse strategies to those used in bilingual families. Language acquisition, in turn, should manifest itself in spontaneous and creative use of L2.

In discussing aspects of acquiring L2 by very young learners I would like to refer to the data gathered for my research on the lexical development of such young learners (Rokita, 2007). In this research project I investigated how much language very young learners of L2 (between 1–4 years old) can acquire in an instructional setting. All children attended the Helen Doron school of English where they obtained 30 minutes of instruction per week. The amount of contact with L2 was to be increased by listening to a course cassette two times a day.

The results of the study clearly showed that the amount of contact with L2 provided by the course instruction was insufficient for the majority of learners to acquire L2. At best it resulted in rote learning of single words, parts of the songs etc., which were also likely to be quickly forgotten. Listening to the cassette did not compensate for a minimum L2 contact either, as it was repetitive and/or incomprehensible, thus the children often treated it as background noise, paying little attention to the meaning or even refusing to listen to it. Thus it is evident that what was lacking was the negotiation of meaning of the language input provided which can take place only via interaction with an adult interlocutor.

The best results were achieved by those children whose parents engaged in some form of verbal interaction/language play with their children at home. In this way, they taught or revised L2 forms acquired in an L2 class, and so provided additional contact with L2. Here it must be mentioned that none of the parents was trained in using suitable discourse strategies. They rather relied on their linguistic intuition and rudimentary knowledge of L2.

Below there are a few examples of such interactions (dialogues) aimed at teaching L2 (also cited in Rokita, 2007).

(1)
Request for clarification

Ada (2;8): Jak jest "piesek"? (How do you say "piesek"?)
Mum (not understanding the question): "Piesek". (Polish – dog)
Ada: Ale po angielsku! (But in English!)
Mum: No przecież wiesz, jak to jest po angielsku. (But you know what it is in English!)
Ada: *Dog.*

(2)
Giving answer prompts

I: Co to jest? (And what is it?)
A: Słonko. (Sun.)
I: A po angielsku. (But in English?)
A: Nie wiem. (I don't know.)
M: Jak to nie wiesz, wiesz. *Yellow* is the... (Why do you say you don't know, you know! *Yellow* is the...?)
A: *Sun.*

(3)
Request for information

Ada (3;11): Mamusiu, to jest *hard.* (Mummy, this is hard – pointing to a window glass on the tram.)
Mum: A jakie to jeszcze jest? (And what else is it like?)
Ada: *Smooth.*

(4)
Giving picture reference; labeling

Teacher: This is a... (pointing to a picture of a donkey)?
Zuzia (2;7): Osiołek.
Teacher: In English. This is *a don...*?
Zuzia: *A donkey*!

(5)
Correcting an answer/facts

Mum: Kaczuszka to jest *cow.* ("A duck" means "a cow".)
Ada (2;8): Nie mamo, to jest *duck*! (No, mummy, this is a duck!)

At first glance these strategies resemble those used in bilingual families (as marked in italics). However, on closer inspection it is evident that these dialogues are hardly naturalistic. The strategies used in them did not serve communicative purposes but were rather aimed at testing the child on their knowledge of L2 items. A peculiar example is the 5th one, not even used in natural situations. Here the parent challenges the child to name an object in L2 by deliberately labeling it incorrectly. Using this strategy, the parent aims to indirectly encourage the child to use L2, as it is a common tendency for all children to refuse to give answers, even if they know them, if they do not serve communicative purposes, but are aimed at testing the child.

What is more, none of those children, even if they managed to acquire quite a few words, was able to combine them in a free novel way, which would be a true sign of language acquisition. From these examples it is evident that the strategies used by the parents of those children did not foster the language acquisition process.

The reason for such use of the strategies was poor knowledge of L2 by the parents of those children. Despite the fact that they used similar strategies as bilingual parents, they also used a lot of code-mixing, and their L2 production was limited to single words. As has been indicated above, children do model their language production on the input they obtain, and the amount of code-mixing they do clearly parallels the amount of code-mixing they hear (cf. Genesee, 1989). Therefore in this case it comes as no surprise why the instructed children had problems in acquiring L2.

In my research (Rokita, 2007) I found only one child who after 2 years of instruction attained a level of L2 competence that enabled her to combine known items in a new, albeit not always correct, way. This indicated that she was acquiring the language rather than learning some items by heart.

Below is an example of a conversation held by the researcher (marked as "I" for an Interlocutor) and the child's mum with 4-year-old, Magda (marked as "M"). They are all looking at photos from a holiday at the seaside.

1. I: Tell me where was it? Where is it? Hm?
2. M(4;0): (silence)
3. I: At the seaside, yes?
4. M: Yes. Here... at the sand.
5. I: Aha, at the sand, yes. Very well.
6. I: And your family, yes? Your family?
7. M: No.
8. I: No? Who is it?
9. M: This is Piotrek, Joania, this is me, this is Robert. (Pointing at particular people in the photo.)
10. I: Aha. Ok. And who are they? Your cousins?
11. Mother: Yes, they are.
12. M: Your cousins?
13. Mother: Nie rozumie tego słowa. (She doesn't understand this word.)
14. I: Ok, kuzyni. (ok, cousins).
15. I: Ok, and what are you doing here? You are here, yes?
16. M: Yes.
17. I: What are you wearing here? Hm... what is it?
18. M: That's Robert.
19. I: Robert is carrying you, yes?
20. Mother: And what do you have on your head?
21. M: A hat.
22. I: A hat. Ok. And were you bathing in the sea? Were you swimming?
23. M: I don't swimming.
24. I: No? Why not? You can't? Can you swim?
25. M: No.
26. I: No? You can't, aha.
27. Ok, but were you playing in the water?
28. M: No.

29. Mother: Yes, Magdku.
30. I: Playing, bawić się, tak? Bawiłaś się? (To play, yes? You were playing?)
31. M: Tak. (Yes.)
32. I: Ok., very good, and where is it?
33. I: You know what it is?
34. M: No.
35. I: And where you on holiday with your mum? Or not?
36. M: (silent)
37. Mother: Magdku: Are we together at the seaside?
38. M: Yes.
39. Mother: We were.

(After a while)

40. M: This is my mummy. (Pointing at the person in the photo.)
41. I: Aah, so your mummy was there, yes? She was on holiday with you, yes?
42. M: Yes.
43. I: Aaah, this is your mummy, you, and this is another cousin... yes?
44. M: Piotrek, Robert, Joasia, a to Karolinka. (Piotrek, Robert, Joasia, and this is Karolinka.)
45. I: Very nice, very good. Ok.
46. Was the weather nice?
47. M: Yes.
48. I: Yes? Ok. And what did you like doing there? Hm?
49. M: Playing.
50. I: Aha, playing. Eating ice-cream?
51. M: Yes.
52. I: Did you eat a lot of ice cream?
53. M: Not, a lot of.

It is evident from the above conversation that the child was able to comprehend quite a large amount of L2. Even when she gave only brief answers, they matched the questions correctly. When the child did not know the answer in English, she remained silent or switched to Polish. This suggests that saying "yes" or "no" (e.g. turn 16, 25) was not an avoidance strategy but truly reflected the messages she wanted to convey.

In addition, the child tried to combine well known items into new utterances (23). She seemed to have acquired such English morphemes as articles, "a" and "the" (line 4), the morpheme "ing" (lines 23, 49) and auxiliaries, e.g. "do" (line 23).

Even if they were incorrect, they reflected the child's emerging knowledge of the language rules. In her language production the child also relied on short-term memory, which is evident from the fact that in order to give a sensible answer she often repeated the interlocutor's last words (53). Similarly, this often led to ungrammatical utterances but was definitely proof that the child was working creatively on the language input she received.

Magda's success can be ascribed to the dedication of her mother who spent an hour daily revising the language from the course as well as extending her knowledge with new structures and vocabulary. Her teaching did not only take a form of a lesson, but was also incorporated into daily routine activities, such as meals, reading books, walking and playing, during which she used similar discourse strategies to those used in bilingual families. First of all, she insisted that Magda understood L2 words, so she did not refrain from translation, and even provided explicit explanation of the form of sentence structures (contrary to methodological guidelines which call for inductive teaching of grammar). However, she also did not accept code-mixing. If the child knew an L2 item, the mother insisted on her providing it (by asking "How do you say that in English?"), and if the child did not know it, she provided the proper equivalent for it. In the latter case she also asked for the repetition of the new item. She also used picture prompts and other cues (e.g. first syllables) to aid the child in naming some objects. Finally, when talking to the child she used the strategy of confirmation check, also modeled in the above dialogue (lines: 15, 41).

It should be mentioned that the mother was a successful self-taught learner herself as her motivation and knowledge of learning strategies must have had an impact on teaching her daughter.

The dialogue is also a good model of what a conversation between a child and parent should be like in order to successfully foster L2 acquisition. First of all, an adult interlocutor must avoid code-mixing. However, he/she allowed to use L1 words by way of explanation when the child does not know L2 equivalents. The conversation must refer to the "here and now" topics. Therefore some picture or object referents are indispensable. The child found it more difficult to talk about more general issues such as her preferences (48–53) or to talk about the past, probably because this concept was not well acquired (35–39). This is probably why the mother used the present tense in order to talk about the past.

Another important aspect is the close bond between the mother and the child which is a necessary precondition for language learning at such an early age. Only when the child has a close and affectionate relationship with her caregiver, is she willing to repeat the utterances or give answers in L2. Otherwise children are unwilling to respond in L2 when they feel the situation is not natural and that they are being tested. That's why the interlocutor must have a lot of patience, give a lot of encouragement and positive reinforcement (praising, e.g. line 46) when establishing a conversation with the child. All these make a parent an ideal language teacher of very young learners. The parent also knows the child and his/her current knowledge of language best, so no one else can tune in to the child's level and provide appropriate and comprehensible language input as well as the parent can.

Conclusion

The aim of this paper was to describe what role different types of dialogue (discourse) can play in child language development, both first and second. More precisely I wanted to indicate why so many early instructed L2 learners fail to attain a satisfying level of L2 competence. The reason is too much focus on single word memorization and subsequent testing, and too little genuine interaction with adult interlocutors. While it is rather unrealistic to provide an adequate amount of contact with L2 and one-to-one adult-child interaction in an instructional setting, it seems a parent, who is a competent L2 user, could be the best L2 teacher of his/her child, using the same discourse strategies as when teaching the child the mother tongue.

Bibliography

Bruner, J., 1990, *Acts of Meaning*, Cambridge, MA: Harvard University Press.

Cathcart-Strong, R., 1986, "Input generation by young second language learners", *TESOL Quarterly* 20: 515–530.

Clark, E., 2003, *First Language Acquisition*, Cambridge: Cambridge University Press.

Damhuis, R., 1992, "Opportunities for second language acquisition of young multilingual children in Dutch infant classes", *Studies in Second Language Acquisition* 15: 305–331.

Gass, S., 1997, *Input, Interaction and the Second Language Learner*, Mahwah: Lawrence Erlbaum.

Genesee, F., 1989, "Early bilingual development: one language or two?", *Journal of Child Language* 16: 161–179.

Gibbons, J., 1985, "The Silent period: an examination", *Language Learning* 35: 254–267.

Itoh, H., E. Hatch, 1978, "Second language acquisition: a case study", [in:] E.M. Hatch, ed., *Second Language Acquisition. A Book of Readings*, Rowley, Ma.: Newbury House, pp. 76–88.

Juan-Garau, M., C. Perez-Vidal, 2001, "Mixing and pragmatic parental strategies in early bilingual acquisition", *Journal of Child Language* 28: 59–86.

Kanagy, R., 1999, "Interactional routines as a mechanism for L2 acquisition and socialization in an immersion context", *Journal of Pragmatics* 31: 1467–1492.

Krashen, S., 1981, *Second Language Acquisition and Second Language Learning*, Oxford: Pergamon.

Long, M., 1983, "Native speaker / non native speaker conversation and the negotiation of comprehensible input", *Applied Linguistics* 4: 126–141.

Newport, E., H. Gleitman, E. Gleitman, 1977, "Mother, I'd rather do it myself: Some effects and non--effects of maternal speech style", [in:] C. Snow, C. Ferguson, eds, *Talking to Children: Language Input and Acquisition*, New York: Cambridge University Press, pp. 109–149.

Pica, T., 1987, "Second language acquisition, social interaction and the classroom", *Applied Linguisitics* 8: 3–21.

Rokita, J., 2007, *Lexical Development in Early L2 Acquisition*, Kraków: Wydawnictwo Akademii Pedagogicznej.

Schaffer, H.R., 2006, *Psychologia dziecka*, Warszawa: PWN.

Swain, M., 1985, "Communicative competence: Some roles of comprehensible input and comprehensive output in its development", [in:] S. Gass, C. Madden, eds, *Input in Second Language Acquisition*, Rowley, MA: Newbury House, pp. 235–253.

Tomasello, M., 1988, "The role of joint attentional processes in early language development", *Language Sciences* 10: 69–88.

Vygotsky, L., 1962, *Thought and Language*, New York: Wiley.

DISCUSSION

Vita Kalnberzina
Riga University
Latvia

The role of language acquisition theories in EFL instruction

The role of parents in first language acquisition is crucial, and most of us have taught our children their first language (with very few exceptions) without the help of any teachers or textbooks. Therefore the interaction between parents and their children during first language acquisition is a popular field of research for both first language acquisition researchers (to understand the mechanism of language acquisition) as well as second language researchers (to single out strategies and compare these with the strategies used in second language acquisition). Lately EFL methodologists are also increasingly becoming interested in this field hoping to improve the EFL instruction.

There could be several explanations for the interest of EFL specialists. Firstly, the amount and quality of theories generated by language acquisition research, secondly the changing role of English, as it is gradually becoming less foreign to more and more people: children watch TV programs in English, they use the Internet sources, play games and listen to the songs in English. This process affects not only children, but also their parents who often use English at their work and are also becoming increasingly proficient in English. Therefore it is only logical that their know-how in providing first language instruction could be transferred to providing English language instruction.

Joanna Rokita-Jaśkow's research on teaching English in Poland to Polish children exemplifies how English can be used contextually, in natural child-parent interaction, where the role of the mother was crucial. The need of parent support in this case of language instruction was only logical, taking into account the scarce contact hours the researcher had with the children (half an hour a week). The role of the teacher of English, in cases like this, thus is not only as a provider of comprehensible input of English language for children, but also and even more so as an instructor of parents who makes them aware of their potential in providing training in English via the same strategies they used when instructing their children in their mother tongue. To be able to provide this kind of parent instruction, teachers would need to have had specific teacher training in first and second language acquisition, which today is seldom part of EFL teacher training curriculum. Maybe it is the time for change?

Agnieszka Nowicka
Instytut Lingwistyki Stosowanej
Uniwersytet im. Adama Mickiewicza
Poznań

Situated identities and interaction learning

Introduction

Conversation analysis (CA) deals with dialogue understood as a social practice of a natural, everyday conversation or a face-to-face interaction. The latest developments in CA extend its scope of analysis to institutional interactions such as: school interactions or interviews as well as conversations in a foreign language used as lingua franca for interaction participants.

In the paper, I address the problem of how interaction participants construe their situated identities in dialogues in English as a lingua franca and how those identities influence the course of an interaction and the possibilities of evaluating learners' interactional competence. The dialogue analyzed in the paper is an interview performed by advanced learners of English as a foreign language with an American native speaker who is also their teacher. The analysis shows that role construction in a dialogue is a mutual process of interaction participants and it is not always the teacher that determines the role construction and that controls topics and turns in an interaction. The results also indicate that the roles learners construe in a dialogue influence their performance, thus they need to be taken into account while assessing their competence in a foreign language.

The paper discusses the possibilities of assessing the development of the interactional competence of advanced learners of English as a foreign language. Using an exemplary case study of a student participating in a two year research, I aim to present the potential of using both conversational analysis and language socialization framework for developing interactional competence as a situated practice. The focus on microactions and identities situated in an interactional context enables a researcher to observe the process of learning in different types of interactions as they are construed by interaction participants themselves. The tentative results point to the significance of individual factors in developing the interactional competence, as respective learners shape their participation, that is their situated identities in a given interactive event, in different ways, thus co-construing distinctive contexts of learning in the interaction. Analyzing the above mentioned case, I aim to show how such constructions of interactive events influence individual possibilities of learning, and to what type of interactional competence they point.

Conversation analysis and language socialization used to evaluate FL learners' communicative competence

In this part of the article Kasper's and Rose's (2002) proposition of combining CA and language socialization (LS) theory is discussed. The main claim is that such a combination might allow researchers to evaluate learners' communicative competence in the way that other methods and approaches cannot because of their lack of good research techniques to focus on an interactional aspect of the competence and on the interactional construction of roles. Since the proposition is far from developed, the conclusions cannot be very determining at this point.

Before introducing the possibilities of such a combination, let me briefly introduce the basic assumptions of both methodologies. The main research focus of LS approach is social interaction, especially the one based on collaboration, as the locus and stimulator of learning (Kasper and Rose, 2002: 34–35). LS focuses on first and second language learning and perceives it as an interactive event, taking place in dialogues between parents and children, experts or teachers or more competent partners and learners or less skilled trainees or simply between interaction participants whose skills differ. It adopts to a large extent a Vygotskian socialization theory, but transforms it and applies to language learning. As one can see, roles and relations significantly influence interaction for learning and thus not only language practice but also language learning. LS focuses on learning discourse so while it also observes learning linguistic or structural elements in the context of face-to-face or paraverbal interactions, it mainly aims to show how interactive context and dialogic roles influence learning discourse. The whole language learning process is perceived as the socialization of learners into communities of discourse practice and specific discourse genres used in such communities. Thus LS provides as well new objects of learning, namely discourse. However, since its primary object of study is learning through socialization, it lacks efficient research techniques to observe discourse. Thus LS could benefit from adopting either CA or other discourse studies. Conversation analysis developed in the United States primarily as a branch of sociology and it focused on observing how the social order gets constituted and reconstituted (Wilson, 1991) in social interactions and what is the shared social order between members of the same society and in an endolingual context. As a result, initially, only conversations in American English as a first language were analyzed. Currently, also interactions in other languages used both as native ones and as a lingua franca are analyzed. Also institutional interaction research of such interaction types as interviews, classroom interactions and psychological sessions starts gaining significance in CA studies. An important and still evolving branch of CA is membership categorization analysis (MCA) dealing with the construction of such roles in interactions as interviewers, interviewees, ethnic others and insiders, doctors and patients, teachers and learners, experts and novices, native and nonnative speakers, etc.

CA seems to be especially useful for observing the learning of interactional competence in a foreign language as it has developed techniques to observe how the social world is constructed by means of the interaction and how membership in second language communities is established (Brouwe and Wagner, 2004: 30, 40). CA based researchers (Brouwe and Wagner, 2004: 30, 40; Kasper, 2006: 83–99) postulate extending an object of learning from acquiring merely linguistic resources such as vocabulary and grammar to developing interactional resources in a foreign language. So CA can contribute to defining objects of learning and evaluating interactional competence, including such interactional skills as: turn taking, repairs and turn shapes or discourse specific actions, as well as interactional co-construction of social and discursive identities.

However, the challenge for CA to be used in second language learning studies is determining whether any learning takes place at all, because CA is anti-mentalist and behavioral and it still, as Kasper points out (Kasper, 2006: 83–99), lacks any theory of learning, meaning the explanation how interactional competence is acquired and how it develops over time. As a result, it can be criticized that it only registers the usage of certain communicative actions and does not prove that actual learning takes place. Learning theory is necessary to determine both the conditions and aims of language learning. In other words, CA needs to define a more specific reference to or invent a learner oriented model of communicative competence in a foreign language and its development, otherwise it will limit itself to observing usages of language.

As for developing a model of communicative competence or at least some model of developing this competence, a concept of distributed cognition may prove a significant starting point. CA's assumptions concerning distributed social cognition and treating interaction as the locus of distributed thinking somehow overlap with LS. Hence, the tentative proposition is either to combine CA with LS or let CA develop its own theory of learning a foreign language based on the concept of distributed cognition. Distributed thinking is based on the minimal unit of analysis in CA, the notion of an adjacency pair, which consists of two parts, action and reaction. The second pair part shows how the first pair part is understood by an interaction participant; this is the way intersubjectivity or mutual understanding is negotiated and this is how thinking in an interaction, distributed over respective and adjacent pair parts, can be observed. The so called "next turn proof procedure" to check how the first turn is understood in the second turn of a pair is the basis to formulate conclusions about understanding and thinking of interaction participants. The analysis either focuses on case studies (meaning single interactions used to explain certain theoretical points) or on a collection of interaction fragments dealing with similar examples which allow to produce claims about the patterns of interaction or patterns of social practice.

LS also observes processes of learning as behavior in social interaction; it claims that learning takes place when children or learners interact with their peers, carers or teachers in specific types of interaction such as for example: "scaffolded interaction" in which a more skilled interaction participant (teacher, peer, mother) helps the less skilled one (by co-producing a part of an utterance along with their partner) to produce discourse just above their average level. While developing a description of communication practices is not the main objective of LS studies, it is on the basis of the observation of those actions, patterns and discourse roles that LS formulates further conclusions concerning learning in interaction. As was already mentioned LS, however, lacks sufficiently efficient discourse observation tools to produce convincing proofs concerning the usage of discourse or interaction patterns and roles in the interaction. It can thus benefit from adopting CA methods.

Situated identities and foreign language learning

Language socialization research frequently focuses on the influence of roles and relations on foreign language learning. Especially, on how institutional roles and relations shape second and first language users' performance in a foreign language. Shea (1994 after Kasper and Rose, 2002: 35) analyzed conversations between advanced nonnative speakers and their North American, native English speakers. The findings indicate that foreign students perform differently in different interactions. The observed student's interactional control over the floor and solicitation patterns, the opportunity to express opinions with authority and hold the floor were significantly reduced to passive confirmations when he interacted with a professor during advisement sessions. As can be observed in the above quoted example, researchers such as Shea (1994) and Hall (1998 after Kasper and Rose, 2002: 37, 40, 45–46) emphasize the critical significance of native speaker's response in construing nonnative discourse even in interactions with advanced nonnative speakers. They emphasize how teachers can shape their students' social status through participation structures and the choice of deictic expressions and interactional routines. An interesting point is that students' performance is strongly influenced by roles and relations in different interactions. An arguable point in such a research seems to be an assumption of putting an advanced nonnative speaker, already in the position of a passive recipient of discourse, while from constructivist (also CA) position such a categorization cannot be assumed *a priori* since categorization is an interactive process in which both students and teachers take part and in which they construe their situated identities.

In what sense are social identities situated? CA perceives social categorization as an interactive process, co-construed in a dialogue and realized in a series of turns. Social categories consist of the collections of descriptions and evaluations, ascribing certain traits and actions to the members of a given group (Mazeland and Berenst, in press; Sacks, 1992). Interpreting a description or an evaluation as a categorization depends on an interactive context, that is how a given description is perceived by interaction participants.

Interaction participants have various linguistic resources, such as most typically adjectives, to describe a person (for example: "friendly," "conceited") (Schegloff, 1972: 88–96). They can ascribe a person to a given type, (also a professional one, for example: "an English teacher", "foreigner"), describe a person's feature or characterize their state of mind (for example: "she's here only temporarily"), place a person on a scale (for example: "speaking English/Polish very well," "extraordinarily sensible"), describe and/or compare their behavior (Mazeland and Berenst, 2006: 4).

In institutional discourse, institutional, professional categories such as teachers and learners, experts and laymen become especially prominent. Such categories consist of certain social actions ascribed to them. Foreign language teachers in classroom interaction have certain interactive rights (Mehan, 1998: 245–269), especially the right to the third evaluative turn in a sequence interaction with the learner and they perfom specific actions such as repairs or understanding check depending on the interactive context of learning (Seedhouse, 1997). For example, the role of a teacher might be realized as the one of an epistemic (knowledge) expert and evaluator at the same time in a pair with a layman/knowledge recipient. This is far from the role of a co-discussant or an argumentative partner engaging in a discussion on equal or semi-equal turn rights.

Research and data analysis

The students' task was to conduct an argumentative interview with a foreigner. The role of the interviewer allegedly allows one to take over and practice the communicative/thematic control and argumentation in an interaction with a foreigner in a foreign language. Yet, a task is never a set up fact but a process realized by interaction participants' interpretation of interaction aims and their roles in it. In other words, despite its assigned name and an academic aim, the interaction format of a task changes interactively from, for instance conversational through scripted formats to a consultation like exchange.

The interview project was accompanied by two types of tasks performed for two academic years of classes :

a. discourse observation tasks (explicit instruction, inductive tasks), in which students' aim was to observe conversational actions and discourse and argumentative discourses (actions and roles) and choose the actions which they considered most suitable for themselves;
b. classroom role plays, presentations and discussions in which students were supposed to use the observed strategies and create observed discourses (roles and relations).

The aim was to develop students' communicative awareness allowing students to find suitable strategies in discourse and finally, develop their personal communicative competence. Kasper and Rose (2002: 49–50) emphasize the importance of explicit pragmatic socialization to develop metapragmatic awareness of pragmatic practices. To be learned or understood, the pragmatic action needs to become salient for the learner whether by means of explicit instruction or during the interaction with the other speaker, usually the native speaker.

The following research questions were posed:

1. How are the situated roles of a learner and a teacher as an epistemic expert construed in an interaction? How do those situated identities influence the language practice, the interaction and thus the possibilities of language learning in an interaction?
2. What are the consequences for interactional competence evaluation? How can learners' communicative competence be evaluated based on their ways of negotiating the situated identities? What are the limitations of assessing learner competence?

The data chosen for the present study consists of a half an hour interview conducted in 2006 by a pair of students, J and Z, with their American teacher W. The focus of current analysis is on J's actions. J involves only in a limited argumentation with W and categorizes W as a teacher and as an epistemic expert, which is visible in refraining from certain argumentative actions such as formulating counterarguments. Such a role construction may be limiting to J's performance and consequently also her language practice. Typical actions J performs in an interaction with W are: active and passive listening, reformulations, repetitions, questions, quotations and topic closing sum ups. She avoids taking up a stance and uses only short metacomments, closing subtopics such as: "that's very interesting ... and what's your opinion." J also refrains from formulating any counterarguments. Certain counterarguments appear on J's part but they are very indirect. She rather supports W, as if siding with a more knowledgeable person by using reformulations that extend and support her interviewee's point against other interviewee Z. On the other hand, W does not contribute to J's categorization of her as an expert. She tries to act as an interviewee and a discussant.

A contrast in J's categorization of her colleague Z can be observed. J categorizes Z as a discussant. She uses more diversified argumentative actions and actually produces counterarguments, taking up a stance as a moderator. J also seems to be more conversational and more confrontational with Z. There is a greater conversational cooperation with Z, especially when she helps him formulate utterances and finishes his formulations for him.

A predominant identity ascribed to W is that of an American English native speaker and teacher as an epistemic expert (might overlap with teacher's role as a teacher usually functions as an expert). I would argue that by performing the above actions J sets up W in the role of an epistemic expert or a more knowledgeable person, since, especially when compared to her interaction with Z, she gives up lots of interactive rights as a discussion moderator.

Fragment 1

.hh and then: eh: : when you are trying to to (.) to: : [go]
J: [mhm
Z: to to the United States (.) .hh n: : : you should: : : (1.0) nh: : : : : : :
(1.0)
J: apply for this visa yeah↑
(1.0)
Z: no but: : °eh° I mean .hhh eh: : : : : you should get in- (.) for example
(1.0) uh: : : : : : : : m a signature

In the above fragment Z shows troubles formulating an argument, which is visible in his hesitations, prolonging words and pauses. In line 5, J cooperates conversationally with Z finishing his formulations and inserting interactive discourse marker: "yeah" with a rising intonation as a comprehension check. This allows Z, line 7 and 8, to reformulate his utterance and make it more comprehensible and listener oriented. In this fragment we can see a greater intersubjectivity, that is negotiated mutual comprehension.

Fragment 2

J: [mhm]
Z: [if you] found eh: : (..) if you found a job (..) than you can go >to
to to< this you know (.) this institution an: d (.) say (..) yes I found (.)

4 the job so you can: : : eh: : : my: :
5 J: mhm
6 Z: eh my visa longer
7 (.)
8 J: but many i- many America: n: : s clai: : m that Mexicans are stealing their
9 vis- eh they are: : eh: : : their jobs
10 Z: you know °uh: : ° I wouldn't say that (.) many Americans (.) are

In line 8 (fragment 2), J produces listening signals and an actual counterargument to Z. The argument is direct, extreme and unhedged. The only modification is that J formulates her utterance as a discussion moderator, voicing somebody else's ("many Americans") opinion. She uses such argumentative actions only when addressing Z. Thus she situates herself as a discussant partner to Z. So does Z in line 10, when he produces a hedged counterargument preceded by a reformulation, using discourse markers "you know" common knowledge reference, hesitation and modality.

Fragment 3
1 J: eh: : : [could you]
2 Z: [and you know] the the (.) the both sides (.) can benefit
3 J: could you be mor: e precise yh: : : =
4 Z: =eh: : (..) for example (.) when the: (..) when a Mexican work (.) legally (.) in the
5 United States
6 J: yeah=
7 Z: =the- (.) n: : they s- eh: (..) he's supposed to: to pay taxes
8 J: oh I see (1.0) Mexicans are: : working for Americans□
9 Z: yeah=
10 J: =and they (.) ha: ve to pay
11 Z: exactly=
12 J: =taxes (..) (where do you work) (1.5) le[gally]
13 Z: [legally] (.) yeah
14 J: .hhh but: : eh: : : m- Mexica- eh (..) America (.) can earn (...) benefit fro: : m: : : (..)
15 .hh eh: : from eh Mexicans (.) but also: : have to pay: : (.) a lot of mo: ney: : (..) on the:
16 m .hh eh: : (.) a: : nd because of: (..) special: : uh: : bilingual' (1.0) project could you s: :
17 : - eh tell us=
18 W: °mhm°
19 J: something more abou: t them

J also uses meta-evaluations or action frames to Z, such as the one in line 3: "could you be more precise." This is a type of an action that assesses the way other interaction participant formulates an utterance or an idea; the way he or she treats a topic. This action, usually argumentative and typical of discussion moderators, directs the topic so in other words, it is a means of exercising topic and interactive control over a dialogue.

She also uses reception, change of mind tokens such as "oh" showing how her mind or state of knowledge actually changed. She does not use such actions when addressing or responding to W, probably because she orients to W's possible evaluator role. In

Polish school interaction it is not advisable to show the changes of the state of mind to an evaluator or an examiner so as not to be charged with the lack of understandings and consequently receiving a negative evaluation. Whatever the reason, the absence of such signals when interacting with W is noticeable. It might be that the teacher in her role is responsible for assuring comprehension in a foreign language. The level of intersubjectivity thus seems to be lower when interacting with W.

In lines 7–13 in fragment 3, J and Z in several speech turns use cooperative formulations and reformulation. Additionally, J somehow "speaks for Z" in lines 15, 17 showing the knowledge of his possible argument and making interactive pauses and looking for Z's compatibility with her formulation.

Such deep level of cooperation does not happen when interacting with W. J only quotes, and reformulates W's words but not in an argumentative or evaluative way. Thus I would argue she construes herself as a potential examiner and an expert whose expertise is to be explored but not argued with or undermined in any way.

Fragment 4

W: the border is a huge area: : : and (..) as Jose mentioned (.) it covers
four states
(.)
J: [yeah]
W: [and] we don't have enough people patrolling this area (.) there's
the[re's]
J: [°mhm°]
W: not enough contro: : l (.) to stop people (.) from crossing the borders illegaly (..)
once they do cross illegally there need to be: : (...) more severe punishments for people
who are caught
(.)
J: mhm: : : so it's like incentive for them (..) to: : t- becaus: : e eh: (.) bo: rder without (.)
guards it is like
W: mhm
J: you kno: : w
W: it it it might as well not be there
(..)
J: yeah (..) that's true and yh: : prison' (.) what do you think abou: : t (.) this' (.) kind of
(.) penalty' (.)
W: .hhhh
J: for them'
W: I think it's a via: : ble option (.) although: : : : : (.) there: : i: : : s: : :
of course the threat that ou: : r prisons

In fragment 4, J mainly agrees with W, thus construing W as an expert and herself as a recipient of knowledge. J does not use as many conversational actions, such as finishing formulations or cooperative overlaps with W's turns. This points to construing an interaction partner as an expert. Such actions directed at W appear only in the context of agreeing with her formulations, siding with W. The cooperation and negotiation level is deeper between disputants in a discussion than between the interaction participant oriented to as a teacher. In teacher's role argumentation is one sided. A person in teacher's role produces arguments and a learner only checks whether she understood them appropriately. This type of an interaction seems to be quite asymmetrical and one sided. Although, as can be observed there is a deeper cooperation when J sides with the teacher or agrees with her. On the other hand, W does not do anything to take over interactive and thematic control. W also cooperatively finishes J's supportive formulations (line 16 in fragment 4). She produces mainly argumentative actions, lines 9–10, which are sometimes very radical and exaggerated in content to provoke J to an argumentative response but to no avail. So the categorization of W in the role of a teacher/expert and examiner and J of a student is achieved predominantly by J, a student. This observation might prove that the critical role of a native speaker in shaping the interaction seems to be quite overestimated in the current research and should be reconsidered.

Conclusion

Teacher and student roles are construed as asymmetrical roles of a knowledge expert and a knowledge recipient. This limits J's repertoire of possible argumentative actions and thus her practice. The teacher role somehow seems to overlap with the native speaker role, since both tend to be treated as experts. The possible reasons for such categorizations on J's part might be emotional, or might as well be a result of her orientation to Polish school traditions which preset and perpetuate such asymmetrical institutional roles for teachers and learners. If the former is the case, this would put Polish learners at a serious disadvantage in interactions with native speakers of English coming from different traditions. Learners' awareness of such orientation could be a starting point of a change. The ability to renegotiate one's identity thus would be a crucial skill in developing interactional competence in a foreign language.

If to evaluate J's interactional competence in discussions only on the basis of her interaction with the person oriented to as a teacher, one could gain a rather biased picture of J's skills. As far as evaluation of competence is concerned, interactional competence (its existence and development) indeed seems to be an interactive and sociocultural process. Therefore one can conclude that the evaluation and development of competence should include a variety of interactive and sociocultural factors, such as culturally shaped participation frameworks (institutional roles and relations). On the other hand, communicative practice should take place in possibly diversified interactive contexts. Developing both students' awareness and interactive resources of the above influences should be the part of interactional competence development.

Bibliography

Brouwer, C.E., J. Wagner, 2004, "Developmental issues in second language conversation", *JAL*, Vol. 1.1, Equinox Publishing, pp. 29–47.

Gumperz, J., 1982, *Discourse Strategies*, Cambridge: Cambridge University Press.

Hall, J.K., 1998, "Differential teacher attention to student utterances: The construction of different opportunities for learning in the IRF", *Linguistics and Education* 9: 287–311.

Kasper, G., 2006, "Conversation analysis as an approach to SLA", *AILA Review* 19, Amsterdam: John Benjamins Publishing Company, pp. 83–99.

Kasper, G., K.R. Rose, 2002, *Pragmatic Development in a Second Language. Language Learning*, Vol. 52, Oxford: Blackwell, pp. 1–339.

Mazeland, H., J. Berenst, in print, "Sorting pupils in a report-card meeting categorization in a situated activity system", *Text & Talk*, Vol. 28(1).

Mehan H., 1998, "The study of social interaction in educational settings: Accomplishments and unresolved issues", *Human Developments* 41(4): 245–269.

Sacks, H., 1992, "Lecture 6. The MIR Membership Categorization Device", [in:] H. Sacks, *Lectures on Conversation*, Vol. I, Oxford & Cambridge: Blackwell, pp. 40–48.

Schegloff, E., 1972, "Notes on conversational practice: formulating place", [in:] D. Sudnow, ed., *Studies in Social Interaction*, New York: Free Press, pp. 75–119.

Seedhouse, P., 1997, "An explanation of the relationship between pedagogy and interaction: the case of the missing 'no'", *Language Learning* 47(3): 547–583.

Shea, D.P., 1994, "Perspective and production: Structuring conversational participation across cultural borders", *Pragmatics* 4: 357–389.

Wilson T., 1991, "Social structure and the sequential organization of interaction", [in:] D. Boden, D.H. Zimmerman, ed., *Talk and Social Structure. Studies in Ethnomethodology and Conversation Analysis*, Cambridge: Polity Press, pp. 23–43.

Woods, D., C. Fassnacht, 2007, Transana v2.20 http: //www.transana.org. Madison, WI: The Board of Regents of the University of Wisconsin System.

DISCUSSION

Anna Niżegorodcew
Uniwersytet Jagielloński
Kraków

Are we ourselves in L2 conversations?

Twenty years of my own keen interest in situated identities and interaction learning makes me naturally interested in A. Nowicka's paper. I find in it my own old fascinations filtered through slightly different perspectives: of the author and of her readings. I also find in it the same research problems I had to face when I tried to apply Conversation Analysis to teacher/student (native speaker/non-native speaker) discourse: its inconclusiveness and elusiveness.

The questions that arise refer to the students' ability (and indeed feasibility) to renegotiate their identities in conversations with teachers and/or native speakers. Should they identify with more open and outspoken English native speaker students, while running the risk of sounding artificial? Or should they identify with their peer non-native group and stay in asymmetrical roles of inhibited learners, while retaining their original identities?

It seems that a gradual change of verbal and non-verbal patterns of behavior in second language conversations as a genuine change of one's identity (e.g. self-presentation as a more assertive person) is possible if students grow aware of the value of particular personality traits, and indeed become more mature and self-directed. On the other hand, superficial repetition of native-like interactional patterns in the English class does not seem to change one's identity. The difference between the two behaviors is like the difference between language acquisition and language memorization.

Goetz Schwab
Department of English
University of Education
Ludwigsburg, Germany

Learning through interaction – a question of identity?

In her paper A. Nowicka focuses on an issue which has turned out to be one of the most promising perspectives for FL teaching over the last ten years: language learning as a social process. Drawing on (Second) Language Socialization (SLS) and/or Sociocultural Theory (SCT), applied linguists have indicated a way to understand the process of SLA from its social contexts. Whether the emphasis is more on language and socialization (SLS) or the process of learning (SCT) is of less importance. Right at the core of both approaches is the idea that language learning is not just an individual process but a common endeavor between teacher and learner, native speaker and non-native speaker or – in more general terms – novice and master (Kasper, 2001). It is understood as distributed cognition unfolding in a "social event", as Nowicka calls it.

But how can we actually get to know what and how people learn when they accomplish social interaction? One way to find out is to take a scrutinizing look at what participants do when they are involved in face-to-face interaction. Due to its in-depth access to verbal interaction Conversation Analysis (CA) has proved to be a powerful means of analyzing discourse in various fields. This close look at face-to-face interaction has unfolded a number of interesting topics. One of them refers to the question of changing identities. Interlocutors do not always take over the same roles, especially when addressing people of different statuses, as could be seen in the paper by Nowicka. Research on identity, at least those based on an interactional or CA approach, could also show that participants' behavior can be related to the general topic of communicative competence, which is crucial for language competence in general.

When taking part in the interactional process of language acquisition, learners perform according to their competences and, at the same time, according to a certain situation shaped by its different participants. Only if we provide a detailed description of it, can we, as Agnieszka Nowicka has done here, give insights into what learning as interaction might be.

Bibliography

Kasper, G., 2001, "Four Perspectives on L2 Pragmatic Development", *Applied Linguistics* 22: 4, 502–530.

Liljana Skopinskaja
Tallinn University
Estonia

The role of critical reading in promoting dialogic interaction

Introduction

Reading literature in the foreign language may be seen as dialogic interaction between reader and text as well as between two cultures – the target culture and the students' culture – within the foreign classroom situation. Due to its dialogic nature, literature corresponds with the need to mediate meanings and interpretations, to establish an exchange of ideas – a dialogue – which lends itself well to the task of raising learners' critical awareness. In Bakhtin's words, dialogue may be defined as follows: "To live means to participate in dialogue: to ask questions, to heed, to respond, to agree, and so forth" (Bakhtin, 1984: 293). It is this type of dialogue that is required in the foreign language classroom if critical reading skills are to be developed.

The present article will first discuss the essence of critical reading through the perspective of dialogic interaction, offering a checklist of critical reading strategies. Secondly, the results of a questionnaire study as well as coursebook evaluation will be analysed about the role of critical reading in foreign language instruction as seen by Estonian teachers of English at upper-secondary school level. Finally, the article offers an inventory of activities that may be employed to enhance critical reading in a foreign language classroom in upper-secondary education.

The essence of critical reading in a foreign language classroom

In foreign language learning (FLL), reading is frequently used for study purposes in order to broaden students' knowledge of the target language as well as their cultural understanding of the target language community. Coursebooks offer texts that are filled with specific vocabulary and grammar units which are learnt within a lesson unit. Very seldom, reading texts require more than fluency, accuracy and understanding of the information presented. Students are confined into answering comprehension questions that do not take into account the deeper meaning that the authors always put into each piece of writing and for which, critical reading skills are required.

Every reading of the text is a new creation of the same text. According to Kramsch, "there is indeed one text, but there are as many discourses as there are readers of the text" (Kramsch, 1993: 122). In a classroom situation, this means that there are a number of dialogues taking place even when learners are reading the same text. Each reader will be a participant in a dialogue, and this dialogue will differ from one reader to another (Fenner, 2001: 24).

It is possible to distinguish between two types of reading: efferent reading (reading for understanding, reading for specific information) and aesthetic reading (reading for aesthetic and emotional response to the text) (Rosenblatt, 1978 cited in Pulverness, 2007: 5). Within these two types, the latter can also be viewed from the dimension of reader – text dialogue. Similarly, McRae makes a distinction between two macro-functions of language – Jakobson's referential and McRae's term, representational, where referential language merely informs, and representational language involves the reader (Pulverness, 2007: 5). Moreover, parallels may be drawn between aesthetic reading (or representational reading) and critical reading, since the learner should pay attention to the underlying intent of a text, and to the ideas and feelings that are aroused during reading, and both require critical thinking from the reader. Furthermore, Brumfit and Carter promote aethetic reading by contrast to efferent reading, saying that texts should be approached in a way that "establishes a personal and aesthetic interaction between a reader and a text" (Brumfit and Carter, 1987: 198). Hence, an important aspect of critical reading skill development is the ability to see a text as the author's creation and to interact with it constantly. Information embedded in a piece of writing cannot be taken at its face value since every text is created with a specific purpose in mind. The reader has to "find out not only what the writer is saying but also why he or she is saying it [...] and what further implications the message may hold" (Altick and Lunsford, 1984: xiii). In order to discover the actual meaning and content of the text, the reader should consider everything with "healthy scepticism" (Aebersold and Field, 1997: 131), discussing, reflecting, making connections, and finally forming his or her opinions.

While reading critically, the reader also makes decisions about the text based upon his or her prior experience as well as cultural background. In Bourdieu's terms, the reader brings his or her habitus and cultural capital, into the encounter with the text, and interprets it from this perspective (Bourdieu, 1994: 12–14). This encounter with the text is a dialogue, which is dialectic and enhances both language competence and cultural awareness (Fenner, 2001: 17).

According to Fillmore, there are three types of schemata that make it possible to make sense of the text and relate it to the previous knowledge: text schemata that deal with grammatical and cohesion structures; genre schemata that pertain to the rhetorical structures of different text genres; and content schemata that refer to the topic (Kramsch, 1993: 124). Canale adds a discourse dimension by including the social and cultural context of production, and the personal and cultural context of reception of the text by the reader (Kramsch, 1993: 124). The presence of such schemata becomes especially important during critical reading since readers who lack any of the aforementioned types of background knowledge cannot perceive accurately the topic or the purpose of the text, or the intentions of the characters in a fictional text.

As far as the suitability of texts is concerned, it should be admitted that critical reading skills may be developed with any piece of writing. However, authentic texts suit that aim better than those which were composed for language teaching purposes. Moreover, Kramsch maintains that as language teachers are encouraged to help their students not only to read texts for information, but also to interpret them for many layers of meaning, it would seem natural to draw on literature as a means of instruction (Kramsch, 1993: 7).

Different checklists of critical reading strategies

In the process of critical reading, learners depend upon their personal background and knowledge. The learners' responses to the text are "the first step toward evaluative reading" (Aebersold and Field, 1997: 130). In addition to the necessity of employing their prior knowledge, students should also be taught to apply critical reading strategies. The information that readers gather as they read, should be questioned and evaluated to see if (1) it fits with their own personal knowledge of the subject; (2) it is presented in a consistent, and logical way, and (3) it is supported by sufficient details (Aebersold and Field, 1997: 136).

A number of suggestions have been made to help learners develop a critical dialogue with reading texts. The earliest set of suggestions by Clarke and Silberstein includes the following questions:

> For what purpose and for what audience is this intended? What knowledge and attitude does the author presume of the audience? Are you convinced by the evidence presented by the author to support the claims made? Does your own experience support the conclusions reached by the author? Do you share the author's point of view? (Clarke and Silberstein, 1979: 56)

The most recent one by Wallace comprises a framework of questions for critical reading based on Kress (1985), which intends to help learners to enter into a dialogic process with a reading text:

1. Why is this topic being written about?
2. How is this topic being written about?
3. What other ways of writing about the topic are there?
4. Who is the text's model reader? (Wallace, 1992: 114)

By asking themselves the aforementioned questions, students will deliberately think about the topic, purpose, and the audience of the text. Furthermore, by employing critical reading strategies, learners will analyse the language choices made by the writer to persuade the reader.

Critical reading demands looking beyond the surface of the text, and the reader should be alert to everything that reveals the true meaning behind the words. Thus the reader should pay attention to the background information about the author: his or her national, historical and educational background; biography; political, religious, etc beliefs and biases; purpose for writing a particular text; and views on a particular topic (Hinrikson, 2005: 26–27). An additional familiarity with the author's background helps to decide whether the author has sufficient experience to make certain statements; it gives hints to any biographical references in the text, or to the topic and the selection of evidence presented.

In addition to the background information about the author, a critical reader should pay attention to the following: the title of the text; genre of the text; structure of the text; date and place of writing and publishing the text; the intended audience of the text; the central idea of the text; points of opposition; diction; speech representation; points of departure; text time compared with story time; characterisation; stylistic devices employed; sentence length and presentation of facts and opinions (Hinrikson, 2005: 27–30). Keeping in mind the title, genre, and structure of the text helps the reader make assumptions about the writer's intent, or further predictions about the purpose of writing. The writer's intent becomes clear when the reader takes into consideration the target audience and their possible biases, and continues to read the piece of writing as a member of the intended audience. Since critical reading involves constant questioning, the reader should pay attention to how the author presents the central idea of the text, or how he or she anticipates opposing views and also, whether the author has any conflicting ideas about the given subject. The choice of words in the text reveals what impression the writer intends to give the reader. As Altick and Lunsford state, words "give us valuable clues to the background, personality, and often the attitudes and intentions of the writer" (Altick and Lunsford, 1984: 52). Furthermore, the way speech appears in the text, carries much importance: the use of inner monologues, direct or indirect speech manipulate the reader to respond differently, and evoke different feelings. The ability to recognise various stylistic devices, or variations in sentence length in the text enables the reader to understand the author's true intentions. For example, short sentences are often employed to create suspension and tension, and are especially effective in bringing out the significant details. In order to decide whether the information given is credible, the reader should be able to distinguish between facts and opinions, paying attention to the supporting evidence and assessing the degree of objectivity.

In sum, a critical reader should consciously look for clues in the text as well as keep in mind the background information in order to reveal the author's true purposes for writing.

Questionnaire study and coursebook evaluation

In order to address the problem of critical reading skill development in the process of FLL in Estonian secondary schools, we interviewed 50 teachers of English at upper-secondary school level of Tallinn and Rapla schools in 2005–2006 (see Appendix). Our aim was to find out the following:

1. whether the teachers are aware of the essence of critical reading and develop it in their lessons;

2. what kind of critical reading activities are mostly employed in the coursebooks and by teachers themselves;
3. whether any supplementary reading materials are being used by the teachers;
4. which coursebooks are most effective for the purposes of critical reading skill development.

One of the reasons for the small number of the respondents was teachers' unfamiliarity with the concept and apprehension to answer questions on an unknown topic. Thus a considerable number of teachers refused to participate in the questionnaire study. Nevertheless, the majority of those who took part in the structured interviews – 79% – claimed to be aware of the essence of critical reading and to develop it at least to some extent through a wide range of pre-, while- and post-reading activities.

At the pre-reading stage, the respondents mostly resorted to the introduction of the topic and class discussion (89% of the respondents), skimming (47%), previewing a text (42%) and listing the existing knowledge (36%).

The variety of pre-reading activities seems to be greater than that of while- and post-reading ones, since the most common while-reading exercise was the critical analysis of a reading text (58%). Other possible techniques were rarely employed due to the relatively limited use of literary texts in the coursebooks. The most frequently used post-reading activities were summarising the content (73%) and commenting (73%), whereas evaluating the evidence and distinguishing between facts and opinions were rarely resorted to, by 38% and 15% of the respondents respectively.

The survey also indicated that although the teachers found the reading assignments offered by both international coursebooks (*Upstream Intermediate*, *Get on Track to FCE*, *Fast Track to CAE*, *New Headway Upper Intermediate*, *Matrix Intermediate)* and local textbooks (*All the World's a Puzzle*, *Focus on Year 12*) sufficient for critical skills development, 78% of the respondents still expressed a desire to work more with literary texts of different genres and to supplement the currently employed textbooks with short stories, poems or plays.

In addition to the above-mentioned questionnaire study, an evaluation of two most frequently employed coursebooks at upper-secondary school level in Estonia – *New Headway Upper Intermediate* by Liz and John Soars, and *All the World's a Puzzle* by Margarita Hanschmidt and Merike Saar was carried out. The analysis shows that neither the international nor the local coursebook contain a sufficient amount of literary texts for critical reading skills development. The reading material offered in those textbooks is mostly seen as a source of declarative knowledge (comprising texts to be tackled as models of foreign language use, or to be focused on content only), and seldom, as a stimulus for procedural knowledge, enhancing dialogue between the reader and the text.

Critical reading activities

Activities that are commonly employed in critical reading instruction are based upon the dialogic nature of a reading text. Since the emphasis is on asking questions which stimulate students to analyse the text critically and evaluate it, distinction should be made between "closed" comprehension questions and open-ended questions. The former being concerned with the surface level of a text do not encourage dialogue, either with the text or peers in the classroom. To stimulate a genuine exchange of information and ideas on the subject, questions need to be open-ended.

The following list presents critical reading activities according to the main phases of a reading lesson: pre-reading, while-reading, and post-reading activities.

Since the activities at the pre-reading stage should arouse interest and get learners to the point where they are ready to read, there are a number of ways to achieve this: by listing the existing knowledge – finding out what students already know, or think they know; by activating appropriate schemata and speculating on the title, genre, illustrations, key words, opening sentences and the conclusion of the text; by anticipating and predicting so that „in a sense they are constructing alternative texts" (Pulverness, 2007: 6). And when students finally come to read the text at the while-reading phase, they do it at a higher level.

The following while-reading activities may be suggested for critical reading skill development.

1) Annotating which helps learners interact with the text throughout the reading process. According to Varaprasad, there are three ways to annotate a text: underlining, questioning and outlining (Varaprasad, 1997 cited in Hinrikson, 2005: 33). In groups of three or five, students may underline stylistic devices, main ideas, supporting evidence in the text, and pass their annotated papers round so that each student adds a commentary to the previous one. In addition, they may note down questions that the text evokes in them while reading the text, so that there is a constant dialogue between the reader and the text. The outlining, on the other hand, helps the reader to separate the most important facts in the text from the unimportant ones.
2) Analysing where students are expected to assess the credibility of statements made in the text, as well as the use of language.
3) "Questioning circle" (Christenbury, 2004 cited in Hinrikson, 2005: 34) which aims at formulating questions about the text being read, keeping in mind the relations between the text (i.e. information found in the text), the reader (i.e. the reader's experience, values and ideas) and the world or other literature (i.e. knowledge of history, other cultures, or other literature). There are four overlapping circles – text/reader (which combines knowledge of the text with knowledge of history and cultures), text/other literature (which combines knowledge of text with knowledge of other pieces of literature), reader/world (which combines knowledge of the reader's own experience with knowledge of other cultures and people), reader/other literature (which combines knowledge of the reader's own experience with other pieces of literature) – that create a dense question area in the middle, which combines knowledge of all three areas into one dense question.

Finally, at the post-reading stage it is necessary to check how well the students have managed to draw inferences and conclusions about the text, have analysed it, and revealed the author's intent behind the text. This may be achieved by evaluating the evidence the author has presented to support his statements; by discriminating between facts and opinions; and commenting upon the text, its subject matter, and what feelings the text has evoked in them.

It is also possible to offer students ways of interacting creatively with the texts they have read. Thus Kramsch proposes a series of variations that learners may experiment with: varying the genre, varying points of view, varying text time, varying the audience, varying the referential world of the text and what she calls teasing out the voices in the text (Kramsch, 1993 cited in Pulverness, 2007: 6). All these variations serve the aim of drawing the students' attention to possible choices which the writer has not made.

Conclusion

In conclusion it may be stated that critical reading has an important part to play in foreign language learning today, and consequently critical reading skill development needs to have a special place in foreign language teacher training programmes. Teachers at both pre-service and in-service training levels need to know how to teach reading in such a way that the reading process becomes a constant interaction – a dialogue – between the text and the reader. The research conducted in this area, the checklist of critical reading strategies as well as the inventory of critical reading activities outlined in the current article serve the purpose of supplying teachers with the necessary guidance for promoting critical reading instruction in the foreign language classroom.

Bibliography

Aebersold, J.A., M.L. Field, 1997, *From Reader to Reading Teacher: Issues and Strategies for Second Language Classrooms*, Cambridge: Cambridge University Press.

Altick, R.D., A.A. Lunsford, 1984, *Preface to Critical Reading*, 6th ed., New York: CBS College Publishing.

Bakhtin, M., 1984, *The Dialogic Imagination: Four Essays*, Austin: University of Texas Press.

Bourdieu, P., 1991, *Language and Symbolic Power*, Cambridge: Polity Press.

Brumfit, C., R. Carter, eds, 1987, *Literature and Language Teaching*, Oxford: Oxford University Press.

Christenbury, A., 2004, "Questioning circles", *English Learning Area*, Department of Education, Tasmania, School Education Division. Accessed through <www.education.tas.gov.au/english/questcirc.htm> (29 March 2005).

Clarke, M.A., S. Silberstein, 1979, "Towards a realisation of psycholinguistic principles in the ESL reading class", [in:] R. Mackay *et al.*, eds, *Reading in a Second Language: Hypotheses, Organization and Practice*, Rowley, Mass.: Newbury House, pp. 48–65.

Fenner, A.-B., 2001, "Dialogic interaction with literary texts in the lower secondary classrooms", [in:] A.-B. Fenner, ed., *Cultural Awareness and Language Awareness based on Dialogic Interaction with Texts in Foreign Language Learning*, Strasbourg/Graz: Council of Europe Publishing/ECML, pp. 13–46.

Hinrikson, H., 2005, *The role of critical reading in foreign language classroom*, Unpublished graduation paper, Tallinn: Tallinn University.

Kramsch, C., 1993, *Context and Culture in Language Teaching*, Oxford: Oxford University Press.

Kress, G., 1985, *Linguistic Processes in Sociocultural Practice*, Oxford: Oxford University Press.

McRae, J., 1991, *Literature with a small 'l'*, London: Macmillan.

Pulverness, A., 2007, "The ghost at the banquet", *ENGLISH TEACHING professional* 50: 4–6.
Rosenblatt, L., 1978, *The Reader, the Text, the Poem: The Transactional Theory of the Literary Work*, Carbondale, IL: Southern Illinois University Press.
Varaprasad, C., 1997, "Some classroom strategies: developing critical literacy awareness", *Forum*, Vol. 35, No. 3: 24. Accessed through <www.exchanges.state.gov/forum/vols/vol35/no3/p24.htm> (29 March 2005).
Wallace, C., 1992, *Reading*, Oxford: Oxford University Press.

Appendix

Questions asked in the questionnaires and interviws with teachers in the survey:

1. Length of service.
2. Classes you teach at upper-secondary school level: 10th, 11th, 12th.
3. Which textbooks do you use in your classes?
4. How much do these textbooks contain reading texts? (frequency scale given)
5. Are you familiar with the essence of critical reading?
6. How often do you use critical reading in your classes? (frequency scale given)
7. If you never use critical reading, what are the reasons for that?
8. If you do, which of the following critical reading activities do you use at the pre-reading, while-reading and post-reading stages?
   Pre-reading activities: introduction of the topic and class discussion, previewing the text, listing the existing knowledge, skimming, other (please describe).
   While-reading activities: annotating, analysing, sociograms, questioning circle, other (please describe).
   Post-reading activities: summarising, evaluating evidence, facts versus opinions, commenting, other (please describe).
9. Do you use any supplementary reading materials to enhance critical reading?
10. If yes, what kind of: short stories, poems, plays, newspare/magazine articles, journal entries, published speeches, other (please describe).
11. If no, what are the reasons for that?
12. Name textbooks for upper-secondary school level that in your opinion contain critical reading activities (at least to some extent).

DISCUSSION

Ewa Bandura
Uniwersytet Jagielloński
Kraków

Rewriting the canon as a form of dialoguing with the classics

Encouraging foreign language students to read critically and to dialogue with the text, as suggested in Skopinskaja's article, is an approach that can be adopted not only in language but also literature classes at both secondary and tertiary levels. Literature in particular gives an opportunity for two types of reading mentioned by the author, efferent and aesthetic. However, contemporary reader's task becomes more complicated when it comes to reading foreign classics, as relating them to the previous knowledge and experience (as emphasised by Skopinskaja) becomes more difficult since it involves overcoming both cultural and historical context barriers. Still, the good reasons for taking this effort were explained in the article. How to motivate the student of English literature to engage ("establish a personal and aesthetic interaction between a reader and a text") with the 17th century poem? The solution seems to be in creating convincing conditions enabling the students' dialogic interaction. The task described below was developed for college students and was inspired by the dramatic quality of Donne's poetic text. This discussion focuses only on the last stanza of the poem. The whole poem is provided at the end of the paper.

> Cruel and sudden, hast thou since
> Purpled thy nail in blood of innocence?
> Wherein could this flea guilty be,
> Except in that drop which it suck'd from thee?
> Yet thou triumph'st, and say'st that thou
> Find'st not thyself nor me the weaker now.
> 'Tis true; then learn how false fears be;
> Just so much honour, when thou yield'st to me,
> Will waste, as this flea's death took life from thee.
>
> (from *The Flea* by John Donne)

After a short introduction to the literary conventions of the epoch and analysing selected literary devices such as conceits and syllogisms, the students were invited to work on their individual interpretations by rewriting the poem as a piece of drama, which meant adding stage directions, describing the setting, naming the characters and ascribing particular lines to them. This approach was taken since I believe, similarly to Skopinskaja, that the dialogue helps to negotiate meaning in search of individual interpretation. Indeed, the dialogue was to take place on two levels: between the students and the original text as well as between the characters in the poem.

The students' approaches are illustrated below with the samples of the concluding lines written by: (1) Ewa Bzowska & Barbara Homa, (2) Ilona Matysiak, (3) Mateusz Kowalczyk.

Different interpretations were revealed by the way they selected most relevant lines, or which thoughts and feelings implicit in the poem were made explicit in the dialogue. Most students could not resist adding new ideas at least in stage directions.

> (1) M: Well… Honey… It's ok. You killed it, that's fine by me, really. It's just another thing that should force you to change your mind. You killed the flea, didn't you?
> W: Yes I did.
> M: And so what? Has anything harmful happened to you?
> W: No… I guess not.
> M: Exactly sweetheart! You see, yielding to me will be just as easy and painless.
> And so the couple is making love. Afterwards, the woman kills the man.

In some cases names were given to characters and the original ideas were rearranged.

> (2) Man: Richard (Dick); Woman: Prudence
> She takes off the sword from the wall and points at the flea with furious hatred in her eyes.
> Dick: O stay, three lives in one flea spare,
> Where we almost, yea, more than married are.
> This flea is you and I, and this
> Our marriage bed, and marriage temple is.
> He grabs the sword from Prudence's hand and they start struggle. Accidentally they both die. The flea has survived and lives on, carrying the drop of the mingled blood, being the only witness, part and sign of their eternal love.

The woman, who is the addressee of the man's monologue in the poem, is given full voice in the dialogue, while the original lines stay unchanged understood as the male speaker's part.

> (3) Woman:
> O, my dear, thy heart has lost its ways,
> I must alone conclude our fates;
> Get away from me thy hands,
> I know where my conscience lies!
> Man (*with resignation and pain in his voice*):
> Cruel and sudden, hast thou since
> Purpled thy nail in blood of innocence? …

Both the choice of language, which was left to the students, and the type of additions they made seemed to reflect the extent to which they could identify with the ideas and feelings in the original text. They either felt comfortable with imitating the poet's style (3), at the same time distancing themselves from the arguments and emotions involved, or found it more natural to use modern English (1), which may result from their closer identification with the character's conflict.

Hopefully, the activity described above would help to advocate the idea of dialogic interaction with the text and to illustrate the points made in the article about the mechanisms involved in critical reading.

The Flea by John Donne

Mark but this flea, and mark in this,
How little that which thou deniest me is;
It suck'd me first, and now sucks thee,
And in this flea our two bloods mingled be.
Thou know'st that this cannot be said
A sin, nor shame, nor loss of maidenhead;
    Yet this enjoys before it woo,
    And pamper'd swells with one blood made of two;
    And this, alas! is more than we would do.

O stay, three lives in one flea spare,
Where we almost, yea, more than married are.
This flea is you and I, and this
Our marriage bed, and marriage temple is.
Though parents grudge, and you, we're met,
And cloister'd in these living walls of jet.
    Though use make you apt to kill me,
    Let not to that self-murder added be,
    And sacrilege, three sins in killing three.

Cruel and sudden, hast thou since
Purpled thy nail in blood of innocence?
Wherein could this flea guilty be,
Except in that drop which it suck'd from thee?
Yet thou triumph'st, and say'st that thou
Find'st not thyself nor me the weaker now.
'Tis true; then learn how false fears be;
Just so much honour, when thou yield'st to me,
Will waste, as this flea's death took life from thee.

Monika Kusiak
Uniwersytet Jagielloński
Kraków

The dialogic nature of the think aloud study investigating reading

1. Introduction

The focus of this paper is the think aloud (TA) study, which is part of a more extensive study investigating reading skills of advanced learners of English. I concentrate on the dialogic nature of this study, as revealed in the process of analyzing protocol data.

In the process of conducting the study, a number of interrelations between various factors were observed: e.g. between learners' first language (L1) and their foreign language (FL), reader and text or reader and TA method. This paper investigates the dialogue between research and theory that became evident during conducting the study, especially at the stage of analyzing data. It explores a symbiosis between the methodology applied and the very construct the study investigates – reading. In other words, the paper discusses how the TA method used in this study influenced the conceptualization of reading.

With regard to the relationship between theory and research, protocol analysis can be used both inductively i.e. as an exploratory methodology, and deductively i.e. in order to test hypotheses about reading that emerge from initial explorations (Pressley and Afflerbach, 1995). Erickson and Simon (1980) and Afflerbach (2000) emphasize the role that protocol analysis plays in the exploration of the very construct it is used to investigate. Protocol analysis may be first used to initiate the construction of theories concerning reading; to break ground for new understandings of reading. It can also direct researchers in their attempts to develop existing theories, facilitating their understanding of a variety of factors that constitute reading.

The main aim of this study was to investigate how students approach texts and what strategies they use in order to see whether there is any difference between how learners read an English text and a Polish text. In this study protocol analysis was applied for exploratory purposes, i.e. to observe readers' behaviors during reading expository texts in English and Polish. However, analysis of the data emphasized the importance of drawing on relevant theories in the process of analyzing data and designing a coding system. It showed how different ways of approaching TA data, based on different theoretical perspectives, contributed to the conceptualization of reading. The next section presents a short history of TA studies, pointing to different conceptualizations of reading that the studies promote.

2. The concept of reading in think aloud studies

Asking people to describe what they think is not a new research method. William James, a famous American psychologist (1890), asked his subjects to introspect in order to develop his theories about human psychic life. Protocol-based research was used to watch how people solve mathematical problems (as carried out by Polya, 1954 cited in Afflerbach, 2000) and how they play chess (as investigated by de Groot, 1965 cited in Afflerbach, 2000). In researching reading, protocol analysis began to be used in the first half of the 20th century, e.g. by Huey (1908). During the cognitive revolution, which followed on from studies investigating human problem solving, e.g. those by Newell and Simon (1972), researchers, e.g. Olshavsky (1976/1977), began to see reading as strategic problem solving.

Nowadays protocol analysis research is burgeoning. It allows researchers to collect details concerning reading and reading-related phenomena. Within cognitive psychology, protocol research focuses on observing single reading-related phenomena, such as generalizing inferences (Collins, Brown and Larkin *et al.*, 1980) or determining main ideas (Afflerbach, 1990 cited in Afflerbach, 2000). Another body of research focuses on what Earthman (1992, cited in Afflerbach, 2000: 167) names "'the concert' of readers orchestrating complex strategies of cognition, knowledge construction, response within acts of reading." Studies focus on acts of reading, as opposed to single aspects of reading within acts of reading (which was the aim of the aforementioned cognitive research). Attempting to describe the totality of the reading task, numerous inquiries investigate more than cognitive strategies; they look at interdependencies of strategies, stances, goals, reader affect and motivation. In other words, they look at the impact of contextual factors on the use of strategy. Studies observe professors and students reading primary source texts in history (Young and Leinhardt, 1998 cited in Afflerbach, 2000) or physicists reading professional journal articles (Bazerman, 1985 cited in Afflerbach, 2000).

A conceptualization of reading as a cognitive process influenced by contextual variables was complemented by studies within the literary tradition. For example, reader response critics (Fish, 1980; Rosenblatt, 1978) view reading as a transaction between reader and text. Studies within this group of research investigate how readers interact and respond to literary texts.

At this point in discussing the impact of think aloud (TA) protocols on the conceptualization of reading, it is worth presenting the synthesis of TA reading research prepared by Pressley and Afflerbach (1995). These researchers examined the theoretical principles that underpin think-aloud studies and aimed to identify aspects of reading that think aloud research investigates. In the conclusion Pressley and Afflerbach (1995: 2) proposed the model of "constructively responsive" reading, according to which good readers are always changing their processing in response to the text they are reading.

The result is complex processing. Pressley and Afflerbach (1995: 117) claim that this complex nature of constructively responsive reading subsumes all processes proposed in the main theories of text processing, namely: reader response and transaction with the text, as conceived by Rosenblatt (1978); monitoring the use of strategies, as described by Baker and Brown (1984); top-down processing as proposed in the schema theory developed by R.C. Anderson and Pearson (1984) as well as bottom-down processing as emphasized by van Dijk and Kintsch (1983); and extensive inferencing, as explored by Graesser and Bower (1990), and an awareness that reading is socially embedded, as investigated by Smagorinsky (1998).

To sum up, think aloud methodology lends itself to investigating a variety of reading aspects: cognitive, affective and social.

3. The think aloud study investigating reading in Polish and English

3.1. Goal of the study

Assuming that students are more skilled readers in their mother tongue than in a foreign language, I was interested to investigate whether there is any particular aspect of reading in Polish whereby students show more skill and which could be transferred to improve their reading skills in English. I considered the think aloud procedure appropriate for this purpose. Gaining insight into subjects' reading processes provides an excellent opportunity to observe how students approach text in both languages, what difficulties they encounter and how they handle these. I believed that applying an on-line method would facilitate a comparison of students' reading in the two languages.

3.2. Subjects of the study

The subjects chosen for the study were five undergraduate students from a foreign language teacher training college: four women and one man – this ratio reflects that of the college population. All the subjects were in their early twenties.

3.3. Texts used in the study

Both texts were authentic news magazine articles: a Polish article taken from *Newsweek Polska* and an English text from *Time*. When selecting these texts no readability formula was used to assess them. Since the study was based on a theory which views reading as a problem solving activity, I assumed that the texts should be somehow challenging for the students. I decided that this challenge should be present not in the topic itself, but in how it is discussed. I therefore looked for texts developing their main topics in an intricate way. However, I hoped that the topics of the texts would be of general interest and that the subjects would find them interesting enough to continue reading.

3.4. Tasks the subjects completed

My purpose was to elicit a natural way of reading a complete text. In order to slow down the process of attending to text, the think aloud task directed the subjects to read texts paragraph by paragraph. This served to elicit reading for main ideas in order to observe how the students construct their comprehension of texts. After each paragraph, students were asked to summarize it and predict what the next paragraph would be about. The aim was to introduce breaks in the same places in the texts and to impose on subjects a similar manner of reading. This was intended to facilitate comparison of the students' protocols.

4. The process of analyzing the protocols of the study – an interplay between theory and research

Below I report on the process of analyzing the TA data. I look at how the analysis of the protocols evolved, emphasizing the role of theory at this stage in conducting the study. The main aim is to report on the symbiosis between the TA methodology and the construct the study investigates – reading.

4.1. Analysis of actions (strategies) students applied

The first stage of analyzing the data involved distinguishing the actions which the students took while reading the text. An individual strategy was considered as an action taken by a student in order to complete the task of reading and summarize particular paragraphs. Strategies were observed as behaviors, i.e. what students did while reading.

A range of actions was identified in the protocols. These various actions were then grouped and named. Below, a few examples of each type of strategy are listed:
Technical strategies – paraphrasing, re-reading and reading aloud parts of the text;
Emotional strategies – expressing surprise, interest, disappointment;
Rational/logical strategies – comparing different parts of the text, linking different parts of the text, predicting the development of ideas;
Evaluating/critical strategies – stating understanding, stating lack of understanding, looking for confirmation of predictions, stating no confirmation of predictions, commenting on one's way of reading the text, assessing the difficulty of the text, identifying parts of the text important to one's understanding, reflecting on the parts of the text.

Technical strategies were the most frequent actions taken by the subjects. They involved dealing directly with the text. These strategies seemed to be the most basic actions that the students took in order to talk about their reading. In emotional strategies, the readers showed their emotional reaction and involvement in relation to the text; they expressed their surprise or disappointment concerning both the ideas and organization of the text. Rational/logical strategies were actions which reflected the students' attempts to manipulate the text. Learners compared or linked different parts of the text to construct their comprehension. This group of strategies also contained strategies that involved predicting the development of ideas. Evaluating/critical strategies entailed actions which showed the critical approach of students to both the text and their process of reading. The students were aware of whether they could understand the text or whether their understanding was not right; they evaluated the results of their understanding, and commented and reflected on it by asking themselves questions about the text and their own reading.

4.1.1. Results of the analysis

The analysis of the students' actions indicated differences between reading in English and in Polish. A greater number of emotional strategies were employed by students in reading in Polish. Students were also involved in more of a dialogue with the text while reading a Polish text, i.e. they more often asked themselves questions concerning the ideas of the text, as if arguing with the text and its author. Furthermore, the results of the analysis indicated differences between individual students in their use of strategies.

The analysis appeared to conceptualize reading as a list of actions. However, the actions carried out by the students highlighted a prominent role played by the text in students' readings. It became clear that it was necessary to account for the dialogue between reader and text in more detail. This led me to the next stage of the analysis.

4.2. Problem/solution analysis

To explore the dialogue between reader and text, the concept of reading as a problem solving activity was accepted (cf. the study by Olshavsky, 1976/1977). The purpose of this analysis was to observe how students approached the texts, and how they reacted to signals in the text. In other words, it aimed to reveal how the students took advantage of the text in constructing their mental representations of the texts. The analysis looked at the mental structures (a set of ideas) that students used to build their models of the text (i.e. their comprehension of the texts). The problem/solution analysis focused on "places" in comprehension which students identified as problematic, and solutions they applied, i.e. how they coped in such situations. The main aim was to relate students' problems to the text by observing how learners made use of texts. Reading problems were defined as the points in students' reporting where students paused in the text and commented on the reasons why they had stopped reading. Very often students referred to these reading experiences as "difficulties"; they said that they did not understand something or found something unclear or disappointing. In many cases, the readers asked themselves questions concerning their reading problems, such as "what does it mean?", "how does this relate to that?"

In this analysis, reading emerged as a problem solving process, i.e. a series of problems students experienced, and solutions they applied to solve them. The results suggested that students' reading comprehension was similar to constructing a kind of system. The readers seemed to develop a construction of their understanding. They were very methodical in identifying problems and looking for solutions. It was interesting to observe how different readers approached the same parts of a text. While developing a coding system, I realized that it was necessary to analyze the text in more detail, and to somehow relate it to the particular ways in which students coped with the text.

For this purpose, the expository text grammar model suggested by Britton was used. Britton (1994: 641 citing Gernsbacher, 1990) claims that "expository texts are intended to build a structure in the readers' mind". The author of an expository text guides the reader by providing: a) the instructions that will enable the reader to construct the correct structure of the text; and b) the building materials, i.e. the concepts and propositions that the reader can use to develop the intended structure. The reader's role is to recognize and execute text instructions; to add any structure building instructions not provided by the author; to use the concepts and propositions provided by the text; to recall and draw upon any prior knowledge necessary to build the structure; and to add any building material not provided by the author. Britton suggests that "the mental structures that readers derive from a text often will be incomplete or incorrect, when compared to the structure intended by the author" (1994: 644). An expository text offers a set of sentences, and the reader's task is to assemble the structure of ideas.

To infer how the students constructed their models of the texts (i.e. their comprehension), two steps were taken. Firstly, the texts were "deconstructed" using Britton's grammar, which resulted in the identification of the main concepts and propositions of the texts, as well as the interconnections between them. Then, as was done earlier, the problems and solutions of each student were identified in protocols.

There was an undeniable advantage of applying a text grammar model to this analysis. It enabled me to look at students' comprehension as a process of constructing a model of text. In turn, this model-based theory of comprehension facilitated an exploration of two intertwining factors involved the reading process: text and reader. It helped to combine an analysis of the text with an investigation of how students read this text.

4.2.1. Results of the analysis

The analysis highlighted that vocabulary and key words were the main sources of problems in reading the text. Vocabulary was an obstacle mainly in reading in English. The students asked questions concerning the words they did not understand. It was interesting to observe how consistent the readers were in developing an understanding of difficult words. Similarly, the readers asked questions concerning their understanding of certain concepts. They looked for links between concepts they found unclear and various parts of the article. They expressed disappointment when they could not find information about the concepts that they had identified earlier.

The analysis revealed that the students were sensitive to certain text cues, for example the main paralinguistic devices of the text, such as the title and subtitle. Also, the pictures accompanying the texts seemed to play an important role in how the subjects constructed their models of the texts. By referring to the pictures, the students developed ideas which had been initiated earlier by means of the text. Additionally, the pictures facilitated an evaluation of student comprehension.

The protocols indicated that the students constructed their models of texts around the key words, i.e. the words that functioned as key concepts in their comprehension. It was important to observe the roles of the first and last sentences of paragraphs in the students' construction of comprehension.

The analysis illustrated how each of the subjects coped with the difficulties he/she encountered, implying that each reader had his/her own "idiosyncratic" way of reading. This finding complemented the similar results obtained in the previous analysis.

With regard to the conceptualization of reading, this analysis implied that in order to obtain a more comprehensive picture of reading, more concern should be devoted to the content of students' comprehension, i.e. students' models of the texts. This led to further analysis of the ideas (propositions) that students formed while constructing their models of the text.

4.3. Analysis of students' propositions

In this analysis, Britton's grammar was applied to analyze students' protocols. For each reader the results of the two analyses, that of the protocol and that of the text, were compared. The results revealed how each reader constructed his/her model of the text (i.e. what ideas they developed in their comprehension) drawing upon clues within the texts.

4.3.1. Results of the analysis

The analysis enriched the conclusions obtained from the earlier analyses. The combination of the analysis of think aloud protocols with the analysis of the text provided valuable information about how the students approached the text, emphasizing the role of text in the process of reading.

The analysis showed how the students constructed their comprehension by interacting with clues in the text. The students appeared to follow some of the clues. However, there were some concepts and propositions provided in the text that almost all the students ignored. The findings raised a question concerning the source of difficulty for readers i.e. which factor is to blame – the author/text, or the reader who is unable to understand the text.

Furthermore, the analysis revealed the students' individual patterns of developing comprehension, i.e. the sequences of their actions. This again confirmed and enriched the results obtained in the earlier analyses. It seemed that each student followed a very similar pattern while reading in both Polish and in English. This implies that there is a transfer between reading in the two languages, probably from Polish into English.

5. Conclusion

In the process of analyzing the data a variety of factors came into play. The findings elucidated the relationship between reader and text. The analysis showed that in a dialogue between reader and text, the subjects were very active, strategically solving problems they encountered. The results emphasized the role of text in students' reading. To explore the interactive nature of reading, a series of analyses was applied. The analysis of reading strategies was followed by the problem-solution analysis, which was supplemented by analysis of the texts. This resulted in looking at both the content, i.e. concepts and propositions of the texts, as well as the ideas that the students used to construct their comprehension of the texts. Combining the analysis of the texts with the analysis of students' behaviors enabled me to see the subjects' reading not only as a problem-solving activity, but also as a purposeful construction of meaning, based on the cues offered by the texts.

In the analysis of the data, a dialogue between the think aloud methodology and the construct of reading became evident. During the analysis, a number of theoretical perspectives related to reading and text were drawn on. The analysis of reading strategies and the analysis of problems and solutions were conducted within the psycholinguistic theory, which views reading as a cognitive strategic problem-solving process (cf. Olshavsky, 1976/1977). The texts read by the students were analyzed by means of the expository text grammar model suggested by Britton (1994), which emphasized the role of text linguistics in investigating reading. I would like to emphasize the role that this approach played in analyzing the results of the study. The use of Britton's text grammar served two purposes. First of all, it allowed me to analyze the propositions of the texts read by the students. It also inspired me to investigate the ideas comprising the students' mental representations of the texts they read and talked about. The process of comparing the models developed by students against the propositions of the texts provided a more complete picture of the reading that I aimed to investigate.

The development of different stages of data analysis enabled me to look at different angles of the same process, thus allowing triangulation. The use of more than one theoretical perspective to interpret the data created opportunities for noticing and focusing on the roles of different factors in the reading of the subjects. This approach underscores the importance of dialogue among different theoretical perspectives in analyzing and interpreting research data.

With regard to the goal of the study (i.e. to investigate reading in Polish and English), the results of TA protocols revealed the following:

1) students demonstrated their own patterns of reading the texts;
2) students followed the same reading patterns while reading both in English and in Polish, indicating that there is a transfer of skills probably from Polish into English;
3) subjects used emotional strategies more often and dialogued more with the text while reading a Polish text;
4) difficulties with vocabulary were more prevalent in reading in English.

To sum up, the study highlighted the complex nature of reading, underlining the interplay of many factors which contribute to this skill such as a L1 and a FL as well as reader and text. In the future it may be interesting to investigate reading from a sociolinguistic perspective, for example by investigating how reading comprehension is developed during a dialogue between readers discussing the same text.

Bibliography

Afflerbach, P., 1990, "The influence of prior knowledge on expert readers' main idea construction strategies", *Reading Research Quarterly* 25: 31–46.

Afflerbach, P., 2000, "Verbal reports and protocol analysis", [in:] M.L. Kamil, P.B. Mosenthal, P.D. Pearson, R. Barr, eds, *Handbook of Reading Research*, vol. 3, Mahwah, NJ: Lawrence Erlbaum Associates, pp. 163–180.

Anderson, R., P. Pearson, 1984, "A schema-theoretic view of basic processes in reading", [in:] P.D. Pearson, ed., *Handbook of Reading Research*, New York: Longman, pp. 225–291.

Baker, L., A. Brown, 1984, "Metacognitive skills and reading", [in:] P.D. Pearson, ed., *Handbook of Reading Research*, New York: Longman, pp. 353–394.

Bazerman, C., 1985, "Physicists reading physics: Schema-laden purposes and purpose-laden schema", *Written Communication* 2: 3–24.

Britton, B., 1994, "Understanding expository text", [in:] M.A. Gernsbacher, ed., *Handbook of Psycholinguistics*, San Diego: Academic Press, pp. 641–674.

Collins, A., I. Brown, K. Larkin, 1980, "Inferences in text understanding", [in:] R.J. Spiro, B.C. Bruce, W.F. Brewer, eds, *Theoretical Issues in Reading Comprehension*, Hillsdale, NJ: Lawrence Erlbaum Associates, pp. 385–407.

de Groot, A., 1965, *Thought and Choice in Chess*, The Hague, Netherlands: Mouton.

Van Dijk, T., W. Kintsch, 1983, *Strategies of Discourse Comprehension*, New York: Academic Press.

Earthman, E., 1992, "Creating the virtual work: Readers' processes in understanding literary texts", *Research in the Teaching of English* 26: 351–384.

Ericson, K., H. Simon, 1980, "Verbal reports as data", *Psychological Review* 87: 215: 253.

Fish, S., 1980, *In There a Text in This Class? The Authority of Interpretive Communities*, Cambridge, MA: Harvard University Press.

Gernsbacher, M.A., 1990, *Language Comprehension as Structure Building*, Hillsdale, NJ: Erlbaum.

Graesser, A., G. Bower, 1990, *Inferences and Text Comprehension*, San Diego, CA: Academic Press.

Huey, E., 1908, *The Psychology and Pedagogy of Reading*, Cambridge, MA: MIT Press.

James, W., 1890, *The Principles of Psychology*, New York: Holt.

Newell, A., H. Simon, 1972, *Human Problem Solving*, Englewood Cliffs, NJ: Prentice Hall.

Olshavsky, J., 1976/1977, "Reading as problem solving: An investigation of strategies", *Reading Research Quarterly* 12: 654–674.

Polya, G., 1954, *Mathematics and Plausible Reasoning (a) Induction and analogy in mathematics*, Princeton, NJ: Princeton University Press.

Pressley, M., P. Afflerbach, 1995, *Verbal Protocols of Reading: The nature of constructively responsive reading*, Hillsdale, NJ: Lawrence Erlbaum Associates.

Rosenblatt, L., 1978, *The Reader, the Text, the Poem: The Transactional Theory of the Literary Work*, Carbondale, IL: Southern Illinois University Press.

Smagorinsky, P., 1998, "Thinking and speech and protocol analysis", *Mind, Culture and Activity* 5: 157–177.

Young, K., G. Leinhardt, 1998, "Writing from primary documents: A way of knowing history", *Written Communication* 15: 25–68.

DISCUSSION

Vita Kalnberzina
Riga University
Latvia

Development of reading strategy awareness

Reading, as a process of negotiation of meaning between the author and the reader, is a fascinating subject of study, involving the existential and linguistic experiences of the reader on the one hand, and the contextual, organizational and linguistic features of the text on the other hand. Psycholinguists focus on the visual processing (the movement of the eye, recognition of the letters and words), syntactic processing (parsing of the text into phrases to establish the links between them) and semantic processing of the text (recognizing scripts and developing schemas of the texts). For a language teacher what matters is the development of communicative competence of the learner and in this process there is nothing more important than the reader's awareness of the processes he or she is going through when decoding the text and its language and analyzing it.

Although think aloud protocol is often criticized in research literature for distorting the authentic reading process, it is an ideal awareness-raising tool as it offers the teacher an insight into how students process texts, what cognitive and linguistic difficulties they experience. The student involvement in the research process allows the readers themselves to become conscious of the complex processing we are all involved in when doing something as "simple" as reading.

The outcome of Monika Kusiak's research, the taxonomy of reading strategies (technical, cognitive and emotional) suggests that when we ask students to read a text, we are asking them not just to use their language knowledge and textual competence, but also their hearts and minds. We should provide enough time and encouragement to enable the students to reveal all their findings and all their problems they encountered while reading the text.

Agnieszka Nowicka
Instytut Lingwistyki Stosowanej
Uniwersytet im. Adama Mickiewicza
Poznań

Research technique as a didactic technique

It seems to me that despite being a noteworthy research technique, think-aloud protocols also have their didactic functions. I have the impression that having the task of thinking aloud while reading, a person activates more metacognitive strategies of coping with comprehension problems.

Another research technique proposed by the author as a development of the research, thinking aloud in pairs about the text, also seems to have a solid teaching/learning potential, especially when used for a longer time. Is seems to me that discussing the text is often a natural follow up of reading it, whether in academic or everyday contexts. Negotiating the understanding of the text in pairs opens up the possibilities of the common observation of comprehension problems and providing mutual help in dealing with them. Besides, discussing the text is one of the activities that resembles "everyday practice" and as an ability involving critical thinking should be the part of the repertoire of every advanced foreign language learner. It seems that developing metacognitive skills also helps readers to understand texts in a foreign language and better diagnose the problems with comprehending them.

The next issue that seems to have a promising research and didactic potential is involving the concept of discourse and discourse communities in reading comprehension studies. If learning a foreign language we do not actually learn only an abstract system of signs but the discourses of a specific culture and society, then learning to read in a foreign language means learning to comprehend discourses. How do discourse type of the text and belonging to a given discourse community play a role in understanding the text? For example, apparently, being even let's say an intermediate learner but the one who is a expert in a given discourse (for example computer science, DJ music) gives one an advantage in understanding the concepts of the text and using more argumentative strategies when approaching a given type of the text even if it is written in an "advanced foreign language."

Leszek Bajkowski
Uniwersytet Jagielloński
Kraków

Before they can teach they must talk: On some aspects of human-computer interaction

Introduction

While promising technological advances have been made in the areas of speech recognition, generation and understanding, developing usable dialogue systems is still difficult as researchers find themselves in need for models of spoken discourse. The models should cover such phenomena as entrainment, turn-taking or dynamic adaptation by providing insight into both human-human and human-machine interaction and their similarities and differences. The work in the field of human-computer interaction (HCI) aids the creation of human-machine interfaces, allowing for spoken communication which is as close as possible to human-human interaction in natural language. The systems developed are designed to assist people with little or no technological insight: a doctor in his medical decisions, a tourist in a foreign city, a customer taken through a display of products, or a machine operator at his place of work. They are also designed to aid a learner in their attempts at mastering a foreign language by way of interaction with a virtual agent. Besides natural language understanding and generation, such agents are being endowed today with other human-like features in an attempt to make them resemble communication between humans as closely as possible. If systems like these are to be viable, they must be able to process spoken language in its many layers – phonetic, semantic and pragmatic – and, at the same time, perform some useful tasks like giving advice, providing information or teaching a language. Each of these inspire a separate field of research in which technical and theoretical problems are identified and attempts to overcome them undertaken.

Chatbots

In the early twentieth century the English mathematician Alan Turing asked the question "Can a machine think?" and devised a test to verify if it really could. If a machine gives an impression that it can interact with a human being in an intelligent way, it has passed the test. It is not a coincidence that the test is based on dialogue. If a human judge who interacts with a machine thinks he is talking to another human, then the machine may be said to think. The famous Turing Test is taken by numerous conversational programs entered for a yearly Loebner Prize competition (http: //www.loebner.net/). A New York philanthropist Hugh Loebner offers money each year ($2250 in 2007) to the programmer whose program called a "chatting robot" (chatbot or chatterbot for short) best imitates human responses. The first chatbot, a program published in 1966 by an MIT professor Joseph Weizenbaum, was called Eliza. Eliza and similar programs imitate communication through a text-based dialogue. They make use of the text input from the interlocutor by applying some simple pattern-matching techniques. The algorithm tries to find keywords in the input and select a response out of its store of responses. As a result if you tell the chatbot "I need your advice", it will respond with "How badly do you need it?" and if you say "I need a new pair of shoes", the answer will be exactly the same. Chatbots are innocent of true syntactic parsing, meaning, pragmatics, and any other linguistic knowledge.

Granted that chatbots have a limited application, they are not completely useless from the point of view of computer-assisted language instruction. First, there is no doubt that even limited exchanges, i.e. dialogues that sometimes go off a cohesive course, can be fun for learners and allow some form of language practice. Second, let us notice that text-based chatbots require the user to enter well-spelled word-forms and, actually, the simpler the text entered (i.e. the more limited the structure and the semantic content of the text), the better chance there is for the dialogue to carry on smoothly. Third, it is possible to download a package of chatbot-building software and even some ready-made content (e.g. some factual statements which will stand for the bot's "knowledge") and write one's own language teaching chatbots using AIML language (some components can be downloaded from www.alicebot.org/downloads/). Also, the teacher can simply use one of the existing on-line bots (a good point to start online is the Simon Laven Page at www.simonlaven.com/). Dave E.S.L., an English-teaching chatbot (www.alicebot.org/dave.html), already exists but requires paid subscription.

It must be remembered that chatting with a simple Loebner Prize contestant is keyboard-based and there are differences between spoken and written language: the inner structure of a spoken dialogue is not the same as the inner structure of a written communication; in spoken dialogue less time is given to language user to formulate the utterance; speech production errors may be corrected; instantaneous error correction and the possibility of making an error introduces hesitation; speech is more broken and looser than writing; there is also some redundant information, repetitions, restarts, interjections, contradictions, and even a tendency to stop the interlocutor (Minker and Bennacef, 2004). Such disfluencies and self-corrections account for 6–15% of what is said. Spoken dialogue is best conceptualized as a cooperative activity to which both partners continually contribute on a continuum from the purely verbal to the entirely non-verbal, involving behavior at three levels: the level of words, the paralinguistic level, and – in some cases – the visual level (Schober, 2006).

Automatic speech recognition

Spoken communication is the most natural and a very efficient way of transmitting language: an average person can type in 20 words on a keyboard, write 24 words on paper, and utter some 150 words per minute (Minker and Bennacef, 2004). There is always an advantage in using spoken language in the accomplishment of a task, especially if compared with using a keyboard. But before systems can converse with humans, the system must be able to understand what is said and it must be able to speak itself. There is no doubt that the research in the areas of automatic speech recognition (ASR) and speech synthesis are well-motivated. In both areas engineers face some serious technical problems which must be resolved before HCI truly resembles a natural dialogue between humans.

Already in 1950s and 60s serious work started in the area of ASR and the second half of the twentieth century marks its steady progress. Researchers from several American, English and Japanese laboratories presented their first recognizers. In 1970s the first systems capable of recognizing human speech were developed and commercialized. Since then there has been a transition from simple dialogue systems to almost fully conversational. Today's speech technologies are commercially available for a limited range of tasks, enabling machines to respond correctly and reliably to human voices, and provide useful and valuable services (Juang and Rabiner, 2006).

ASR technology is the process of converting incoming phone strings into a sequence of known words. Discrete speech recognizers require that the speaker use discrete speech by introducing pauses of about 200 msec in between the words. This is an unnatural manner of speaking, tedious and difficult to learn but with respect to CALL the solution may be preferred for some applications where practice in the pronunciation of separate words or sounds is the primary goal. With respect to continuous speech, two major approaches to ASR can be well represented by the efforts of IBM and AT&T Bell Laboratories leading, respectively, to creating two types of ASR systems: speaker-dependent and speaker-independent. Since IBM wanted to develop a voice-activated typewriter performing transcription, they developed a speaker-dependent tool that needs to be trained; namely, the user must spend some time reading words and short texts to teach the system about his voice characteristics. A user-trained system can generally cover a large vocabulary at normal pace with a high accuracy. On the other hand, AT&T was after an automated telecommunication public service expected to work well for millions of talkers. Speech recognition algorithms were based on an acoustic model (spectral representation of sounds or words). The acoustic model is trained on a corpus of audio samples. The audio recordings are transcribed and then a statistically represented as speech models. The result is a speaker-independent system which can recognize a smaller number of words but accept input from many different speakers, often with notably different accents. Speech recognition research in the 1980s was characterized by a shift in methodology from the more intuitive template-based approach (templates were recorded patterns to which input was matched) toward a more rigorous statistical modeling framework. Thus while technology was realized differently in various applications, the statistical methods caused a certain degree of convergence in the system design. Most notably the method known as Hidden Markov Model, which measures the probability of the next element in a string, has been wildly implemented (Juang and Rabiner, 2006).

Accuracy of ASR systems has always been constrained by practical factors such as background noise, accent, sound card quality, pre-amplifying, microphone type and placement, fatigue and stress of users induced by the task or type of utterance. Various methods were tried in response to the problem of corrupted input. In one method, called keyword spotting, the presence of a key-phrase is sufficient to indicate the caller's intent so that the system can trigger an appropriate response. This simple substitute of semantic understanding generally works well because the vocabulary used in the context is limited and therefore less ambiguous than in free dialogue. Systems that employ ASR are designed to allow humans to converse with a database containing information about some specific domain. They are also geared towards performing specific tasks (e.g. providing information about hotels or tutoring about physics) and the HCI takes place in a specific context where the users are expected to conform to linguistic conventions (in a way, there is a limited set of ways to, say, ask about the train times). Therefore the ASR systems are mostly task-oriented and domain-specific.

From the perspective of CALL the most important consideration is how effective the ASR techniques actually are. The performance of ASR systems is specified in terms of accuracy (word error rate) and speed, measured with the real time factor, i.e. how much time is needed to process a recording of a certain duration. Manufacturers generally provide prospective buyers with very high accuracy figures in the range between 95–99%. With respect to the early systems, the claim was verified in a series of laboratory experiments and the researchers reported it was nearer 70%. The answer is in fact always technology-dependent and always related to the human-machine interface design. Also, according to Lamel and Gauvain (2003), tasks should be divided according to which error rates are measured. In small vocabulary tasks (isolated common words) the error rate is below 1%; for read speech tasks (approximately 1000 words) the rate is 3%; and for large vocabulary tasks word-error rates around 8% were obtained using a 65k vocabulary (the data come from 1995, the texts read to the system were newspaper articles from the *Wall Street Journal*). The tasks are different and yield a wide range of results. It is difficult to compare results across the systems; besides, benchmarks for many of the contemporary systems are not publicly available. The best accuracy reported in 1990s with respect to "raw" recognition of continuous speech (e.g. recognition of texts from the *New York Times* read by humans) was 95%, i.e. one recognition error in every twenty words (Ehsani and Knodt, 1998).

Automatic speech generation

Parallel to ASR, speech generation has developed driven by the same technological developments. Today the technology is mainly used in the task of text-to-speech synthesis (TTS), i.e. converting text (of unrestricted vocabulary) into intelligible speech, but building machines that can imitate human ability to talk has a long history that starts with purely mechanical devices. In the eighteenth century inventors like Kretzenstein, Von Kempelen or Wheatstone tried to build acoustic speaking machines. The technological milestone of the first half of the twentieth century was Homer Dudley's speech synthesizer called the VODER, which was demonstrated in New York in 1939. In 1961 Bell Laboratories showed a computer-based speech synthesis system, a demonstration seen by the author Arthur C. Clarke, giving him the inspiration for the talking computer HAL in "2001: A Space Odyssey". Application potential of synthetic speech is enormous. Speech synthesis provides important utility in situations where a person's eyes and hands are busy, they are used extensively by telecommunication industry or in devices that read out loud for the blind, in video games or children's toys or provide voice for sufferers of neurological disorders: for example, the physicist Stephen Hawking used DECtalk developed by Dennis Klatt.

There are three methods used to generate synthetic speech: concatenative, formant, and articulatory synthesis. Most modern commercial TTS systems are based on concatenative synthesis, in which samples of speech are chopped up, stored in a database, and combined and reconfigured to create new sentences. In terms of its quality, today's synthetic speech is nearing the level of natural speech but it is still not equivalent to it. Its perception and comprehension are still worse than natural speech, and it degrades faster under adverse listening conditions (e.g., noise, distraction, divided attention). Besides, when tasks are demanding, the ability to understand synthetic speech is adversely affected (for example, pilots reported not hearing any synthesized warning sounds or messages when they were in a dangerous situation). Conversely, the more experience a listener has with a particular text-to-speech system, the higher the intelligibility of the speech (for example, blind programmers who routinely used a low-intelligibility synthesizer called Votrax Type-'n-Talk reported that the speech quality improved substantially). Some improvements in the field have come from the work with prosodic rules (like stress or pitch contour) which adjust pronunciations to contexts. Other solutions could be provided by work on affective features, a technology known as emotional speech. By adding emotional quality to synthesized voice, affective information is added and, as a consequence, unnaturalness reduced. Emotional speech synthesis is also important for the use of synthetic speech as prosthesis for voice-disabled individuals that need to rely on synthetic speech for conveying the same range of information conveyed by human speech (Jurafsky and Martin, 2006; Nusbaum and Shintel, 2006).

Talking heads and pedagogical agents

Many of today's instructional tutoring systems incorporate both the speech recognition and generation components, in which case the latter carries the auditory model of the foreign language. This can be significantly enhanced by a variety of visual aids. A very good example of a successful technology using visual enhancement is Baldi, a part of CSLU Speech Toolkit (http: //www.cslu.edu/toolkit/) – an authoring environment for building spoken language systems. It includes recognition modules, text-to-speech synthesis and facial animation in the form of a 3-D "talking head", which provides realistic speech organs movements synchronized with the audio. The user of this software can see the speech organs and how they move to produce a particular sound. The animation technology allows to visualize processes giving the kind of insight that is not possible even with a living human being. The motivation behind this technology is the audio-visual speech studies reinvigorated by McGurk and MacDonald (1976). They demonstrated that seeing the face of the speaker influences the way we hear the sound. The creators of Baldi consider speech not just an auditory but a multimodal phenomenon. Perception and understanding are not only enhanced by a speaker's face and gestures: visual and auditory speech are complementary (one of the sources is strong when the other is weak) and there is an optimal integration of the two sources of information. The animated face can be aligned with the output of a speech synthesizer or natural auditory speech. It also allows synthesis of several other languages except English, such as Spanish, Arabic, Chinese, German, and Russian. Other studies also demonstrated the influence of vision on audition. For example, it has been estimated that seeing the talker offers a gain equivalent to around a 15 dB increase in signal-to-noise ratio for users of English. What the face talking to you looks like also seems to have an effect on speech perception: talkers who appear to be Japanese generate different effects than those who appear to be American (Campbell, 2006; Massaro *et al.*, 2006).

"Talking heads" have been used as language tutors for both native and second-language learners and individuals with special needs. In experiments evaluating the effectiveness of the tool, the fact exploited most was the multiplicity of sources of information in perception, recognition, learning, and retention. Researchers put emphasis on the fact that words are experienced from many different perspectives: the learner observes them being spoken by a realistic-looking talking head, sees them in writing, sees visual images of referents of the words, types them, hears him- or herself say the words, and compares them with the correct pronunciation of words used in context. The experiments showed that the application could be used successfully with reading-impaired and autistic children, children with hearing loss, and regular English language learners alike to teach new vocabulary (Massaro *et al.*, 2006).

Visualization embedded in the system interface allows for a two-way multi-modal contact between the user and the system. Unlike direct manipulation interfaces, intelligent, interactive, animated pedagogical agents offer an ease of access to the system (Brennan, 1998). Since they take the shape of a 2-D or 3-D character and are often placed in a virtual environment, they can be seen and addressed. They can demonstrate principles, procedures and actions; they can use gestures, gaze and other visual aids to teach but also to attract the student's attention or regulate turn-taking in a mixed-initiative dialogue. Head nods and facial expressions, which are natural devices present in a human dialogue, can provide unobtrusive feedback on the student's utterances and actions. The mere presence of a lifelike agent may increase the student's motivation to perform the task well. While animated pedagogical agents increase the computer's ability to engage and motivate students, there are also quite a lot of things they should be able to do. They need to give the user an impression of being knowledgeable, attentive, helpful, or concerned. In short, they should look believable enough to support pedagogical interactions. Besides, pedagogical agents must exhibit flexibility in order to manage the learning environment and the student, with their unpredictable aptitudes, levels of proficiency, and learning styles. All this means that the implemented model must be dynamic and adaptive, as opposed to deliberate, sequential, or preplanned.

Managing human-machine dialogue

Of course to recognize words and sentences and generate human-like voice is one thing; making a conversation is another. Speech applications which support spontaneous and conversational styles often require a dialogue between the user and the machine to reach some desired state of understanding. Such a dialogue often requires such operations as query and confirmation, thus making some allowance for errors and repairs. These factors focused the attention of the research community on the dialogue management component. MIT's Pegasus and Jupiter and the HMIHY (which stands for How May I Help You?) developed at AT&T are noteworthy for their ability to manage dialogue effectively. Pegasus provides information about the status of airline flights; Jupiter can be asked about the weather conditions (Juang and Rabiner, 2006).

Dialogue management seems to be the key to successful virtual tutoring. A convincing dialogue system must be able to maintain a pragmatically appropriate conversation which includes the ability to handle semantic trickiness (e.g. anaphors, ellipses or synonymy), identify the topic, use backchannels, know when to take turns, or establish common ground. In CALL settings it should also have some sort of mechanism to control the task completion and provide feedback. Some effort towards using dialogue systems for language instruction has already been made. After adapting a telephone-based bus schedule information system called Let's Go for CALL (for speech recognition and correction prompt generation) Raux and Eskenazi (2004) conclude that it can be used to provide realistic, involved environment for language learning. They say there is potential for CALL in those systems as they place the student in a realistic situation where a specific task has to be accomplished in the target language. Unfortunately, such systems assume that the users' language is perfect and any disruption is due to speech recognition errors on the part of the machine and therefore some acoustic and lexical improvements have to be made.

Today's language teaching systems, for example Herr Kommissar, Subarashii, Virtual Conversations or TLTS, analyze pronunciation or teach speaking through games or role play (Johnson *et al.*, 2004), but they do not support a fully complex open-ended dialogue. Subarashii and Steve are good examples of existing virtual tutors. Subarashii is a language tutor used to teach beginner's Japanese through virtual spoken interactions by role play (like inviting a friend to the cinema). An animated agent takes one of the roles in the dialogue. It is designed to understand what a student says and respond in a meaningful way in spoken Japanese. Although the student is not directly presented with a list of response choices, the exercises are constrained because the expected responses are still limited to a few correct ones. Despite the restricted communicative competence of second language beginners, the range of utterances, both valid and invalid, which they can produce is huge. Subarashii successfully processes all correct utterances but also recognizes and rejects many incorrect ones. Experiments with students in California have shown that "ASR works in a school setting, and that high school students seem to enjoy it" (Bernstein *et al.*, 1999).

While the Subarashii interlocutors are 2-D animated persons, Steve (Soar Training Expert for Virtual Environments) can be seen by the student in stereoscopic 3-D. The agent can also see the student thanks to the virtual environment's tracking hardware which monitors the student's position and orientation in the environment. More importantly, however, it is designed to interact within the virtual environment. Steve can adapt his demonstrations in midstream if the student performs actions that interact with the demonstration and respond to student interruptions. Steve has been applied to naval training tasks such as operating the engines aboard US Navy ships. The authors say that the immaturity of the technology prevents any comprehensive, definite empirical studies of the effectiveness of animated pedagogical agents. However, they quote a study conducted with one hundred middle school students the purpose of which was to obtain a "baseline" reading of the effectiveness and impact of various forms of agent advice. The primary conclusion was that students interacting with learning environments with an animated pedagogical agent show "statistically significant increases from pre-tests to post-tests" (Johnson *et al.*, 2000).

Systems like Let's Go, Subarashii or Steve cannot handle a completely unconstrained spoken conversation, and other systems which attempt to do so generally fail (Jurafsky and Martin, 2000). The issue, as it seems, is the lack of applicable models of interaction. These models are being sought and dialogue is being analyzed with respect to both human-human and human-machine interaction. Because computer talk (another label for HCI, by analogy to "baby talk") reveals some features that are replicated and observable again and again, the conclusion is that there exists a regular register for humans conversing with dialogue systems. Here are some reasons why HCI is not a simple replication of regular dialogue: in communication with the machine, apart from its manifestly task-oriented and domain-specific character, people display a range of adaptive language behaviors (Minker and Bennacef, 2004; Leech and Weisser, 2003). The adaptation is similar to that found in human-human communication but it also has its peculiarities.

Cooperation through alignment

One way people change their behavior in the course of a dialogue – alignment – has been intensively studied in the context of HCI. In the cooperation process people try to align with the conversation through back-channeling (responses like "yes", "hmmm", "I see", "uh-huh", facial expressions, eye-contact, nods and gestures), common ground (sharing knowledge, sentiments, associations), and some social factors (such as talking to a child or a superior). The tendency to align is most vivid in entrainment, a cooperative reuse of each other's language. Garrod and Anderson (1987 cited in Porzel, 2006) suggest that people tend to automatically converge on lexical and syntactic choices via a low-level mechanism of interpersonal priming. The hypothesis is that the participants attempt to align their situation models, i.e. their common understanding of the situation. At a lexical level alignment is achieved through the choice of words out of the vocabulary used by the interlocutor. The one who introduces a term is denoted as the leader and the one who adopts it as the follower. First, the interlocutors need to establish common ground for their conversation. After that they hedge, i.e. they mark the term as provisional, pending evidence of acceptance from the other. Only then do they agree on the same choice of words. As a last step, the terms are no longer indefinite and can be shortened, e.g. via anaphora, pronominalization or gapping (Porzel, 2006). Brennan (1996), who explored conceptual pacts people make during conversation, says that the shared conceptualization between interlocutors is marked by using the same terms to refer to the same objects. While the likelihood that people in one conversation would choose the same terms for the same common object as people in another conversation is only 10%, in a situation when two people repeatedly discuss the same object, they come to use the same terms and stay with them for the rest of the dialogue. Brennan (1996) has also shown that people will align their language towards that of computer agents.

In the case of HCI, the users' lexical choice seems to be strongly influenced by their beliefs and expectations about the system. Pearson *et al.* (2006) report that when users believe that the system is unsophisticated and restricted in capability, they adapt their language to match the system's language more than when they believe the system is relatively sophisticated and capable. Interestingly, the actual behavior of the system is irrelevant. Bhatt *et al.* (2004) studied student use of hedges (expressions like "I guess", "maybe", "kind of", "I'm not sure", etc.) and affect (present in expressions like "sorry", "wow", "I get it", "I'm a bit confused") in interacting with both humans and computer systems, during keyboard-mediated natural language tutoring sessions in medicine. They say that while hedging always occurred in human-human dialogues, there was virtually no hedging when subjects addressed machines. As opposed to hedging, students do express affect to machines, though far less often than to humans. They do not apologize or thank or give computers direct feedback; they do, however, express confusion, frustration and even rage. The conclusion is that students who know they are interacting with a computer change their attitude towards the conversation, and they are less concerned with helping to keep the flow going than they are in regular conversation. Other authors have come to similar conclusions: in a dialogue with a machine, humans change their attitude. But they may act reasonably if prompted to do so. This is illustrated by the issue of turn-taking behavior of "naive users", i.e. persons who communicate with the system without any or with too little prior experience to adjust linguistic behavior. These are situations where the human interlocutor makes an additional or second utterance before the system has provided its response to the first utterance. After that the conversation becomes asynchronous; the system responds to the last but one utterance while in the user's mind that response concerns the last. In consequence, the dialogue fails completely. Clearly, conversational dialogue systems suffer from a lack of strategies that would prevent the dialogue from becoming "out of sync" and allow repairs (Porzel, 2006). However, this may be remedied by the dialogue management component which should keep the user informed about the process and provide messages telling him to stand by or restart (e.g. "I listen to you, please go on").

Conclusion

There is no denying that technology has made huge advances in the recent years in such areas as speech synthesis and recognition, visualization, and pragmatically motivated dialogue control. The hope is that many of the partial capacities of various state-of-the-art systems will be eventually put together to make a system that can actually engage in a sensible conversation and teach a language in a technologically unconstrained fashion. A review of literature and online resources shows that there are still many features of human speech that are problematic and machines passing the Turing Test are not imminent, but as technology continues to mature, the number of valuable systems that become part of our daily life is growing. At the same time some frustration is visible concerning the missing theoretical background in terms of a clear account of the nature of human-human, human-computer (and recently also computer-human) interaction that would allow systems designers to look for engineering solutions. As for CALL-oriented applications, there is always a need for empirically verified knowledge about their effectiveness in real learning context. Some grounds, however, exist to believe that, once useful interaction models are available and technical hurdles disappear, teachers and learners may obtain effective and attractive technological support to complement their human effort in the area of language teaching.

Bibliography

Bernstein, J., A. Najmi, F. Ehsani, 1999, "Subarashii: encounters in Japanese spoken language education", *CALICO Journal* 16 (3): 361–384. Accessed through <www.calico.org/html/article_619.pdf> (10 August 2007).

Bhatt, K., M. Evans, S. Argamon, 2004, "Hedged responses and expressions of affect in human/human and human/computer tutorial interactions". Accessed through <lingcog.iit.edu/doc/bhattevansargamonsubmit.pdf> (10 August 2007).

Brennan, S.E., 1996, "Lexical entrainment in spontaneous dialog", *International Symposium on Spoken Dialog ISSD-96*, 41–44. Accessed through <www.psychology.sunysb.edu/ sbrennan-/papers/brenissd.pdf> (10 August 2007).

Brennan, S.E., 1998, "The grounding problem in conversations with and through computers", *Social and Cognitive Psychological Approaches to Interpersonal Communication*, 201–225, Hillsdale, NJ: Lawrence Erlbaum. Accessed through <www.psychology.sunysb.edu/sbrennan-/papers/brenfuss.pdf > (10 August 2007).

Campbell, R., 2006, "Audio-visual speech processing", [in:] K. Brown, ed., *Elsevier Encyclopedia of Language and Linguistics*, Oxford: Elsevier Ltd, pp. 562–569. Accessed through <www.uj.edu.pl> (2 March 2007).

Ehsani, F., E. Knodt, 1998, "Speech technology in computer-aided language learning: strengths and limitations of a new CALL paradigm", *Language Learning and Technology* 2(1): 45–60. Accessed through <llt.msu.edu/vol2num1/article3/> (10 March 2007).

Garrod S., A. Anderson., 1987, "Saying what you mean in dialogue: A study in conceptual and semantic coordination", *Cognition* 27: 181–218.

Johnson, W.L., J.W. Rickel, J.C. Lester, 2000, "Animated pedagogical agents: face-to-face interaction in interactive learning environments", *International Journal of Artificial Intelligence in Education* 11: 47–78. Accessed through <www.isi.edu/isd/carte> (12 August 2007).

Johnson, L., S. Choi., S. Marsella, N. Mote, S. Narayanan, H. Vilhjlmsson, S. Wu, 2004, "Tactical language training system: supporting the rapid acquisition of foreign language and cultural skills", *Proceedings of InStil*, July 2004. Accessed through <sail.usc.edu/publications/TLTS-InSTIL-General.pdf> (15 August 2007).

Juang, B.H., L.R. Rabiner, 2006, "Automatic Speech Recognition-A Brief History of the Technology", [in:] K. Brown, ed., *Elsevier Encyclopedia of Language and Linguistics*, Oxford: Elsevier Ltd, pp. 806–819. Accessed through <www.uj.edu.pl> (2 March 2007).

Jurafsky, D., J.H. Martin, 2000, *Speech and Language Processing: An Introduction to Natural Language Processing, Computational Linguistics, and Speech Recognition*, New Jersey: Prentice Hall. Accessed through <www.cs.colorado.edu/~martin/SLP/slp.html> (10 June 2007).

Lamel, L., L. Gauvain, 2003, "Speech Recognition", [in:] R. Mitkov, ed., Oxford Handbook of Computational Linguistics, Oxford: Oxford University Press, pp. 305–322.

Leech, G., M. Weisser, 2003, "Pragmatics and Dialogue", [in:] R. Mitkov, ed., *Oxford Handbook of Computational Linguistics*, Oxford: Oxford University Press, pp. 136–156.

Massaro, D.W., Y. Liu, T.H. Chen, C.A. Perfetti, 2006, "A multilingual embodied conversational agent for tutoring speech and language learning", *Proceedings of the Ninth International Conference on Spoken Language Processing*, Bonn: Universität Bonn, pp. 825–828. Accessed through <mambo.ucsc.edu/pdf/massarobox.pdf> (28 July 2007).

McGurk, H., J. MacDonald, 1976, "Hearing lips and seeing voices", *Nature*, vol. 264 (5588), 746–748.

Minker, W., S. Bennacef, 2004, *Speech and Human-Machine Dialog*, Boston: Kluwer Academic Publishers.

Nusbaum, H.C., H. Shintel, 2006, "Speech Synthesis", [in:] K. Brown, ed., *Elsevier Encyclopedia of Language and Linguistics*, vol. 12, Oxford: Elsevier Ltd, pp. 19–30. Accessed through <www.uj.edu.pl> (2 March 2007).

Pearson, J., Hu Jiang, H.P. Branigan, M.J. Pickering, C.I. Nass, 2006, "Adaptive language behavior in HCI: how expectations and beliefs about a system affect users' word choice", *Conference on Human Factors in Computing Systems*, pp. 1177–1180. Accessed through <portal.acm.org> (10 June 2007).

Porzel, R., 2006, "How computers (should) talk to humans". *How People Talk to Computers, Robots, and other Artificial Communication Partners. Proceedings of the Workshop Hansewissenschaftskolleg*, April 21–23. Accessed through <nats-www.informatik.uni-hamburg.de/~fischer/hriproc.pdf> (10 June 2007).

Raux, A., M. Eskenazi, 2004, "Using Task-Oriented Spoken Dialogue Systems for Language Learning: Potential, Practical Applications and Challenges", *InSTIL* 2004, Venice, Italy. Accessed through <www.cs.cmu.edu/~antoine/papers/rauxeskenazi-instil-04.pdf> (12 June 2007).

Schober, M.F., 2006, "Dialogue and Interaction", [in:] K. Brown, ed., *Elsevier Encyclopedia of Language and Linguistics*, Oxford: Elsevier Ltd, pp. 562–571. Accessed through <www.uj.edu.pl> (2 March 2007).

DISCUSSION

Jarosław Krajka
Uniwersytet Marii Curie-Skłodowskiej
Lublin

On some aspects of teacher-computer interaction

In the Polish EFL setting, with non-native teachers of English with often imperfect pronunciation, there arises a frequent need to seek ways of enhancing the impact of language instruction, implementing modern technological tools to compensate for non-native speaker teachers' shortcomings. It seems the Human-Computer Interaction tools described in the paper, such as Automatic Speech Recognition (ASR), Automatic Speech Generation (ASG) and Talking Agents, might give a new dimension to teaching pronunciation, especially in its phases of articulation presentation, discrimination and practice.

My experiences with introducing some of these solutions in teacher training were quite promising – online demonstration versions of Text-to-Speech synthesis programs were used by teacher trainees to generate foreign sounding text to expose the peculiarities of the "English-by-Poles" accent, while Baldi, the Talking Agent, was implemented as one of the devices to assist articulation presentation. While many of the tools described in the paper are generally complex and beyond the reach of an ordinary language teacher, focus on selected functionalities or their online demonstration counterparts (if available) could allow increasing impact keeping teacher education economy at the same time.

Strikingly enough, the major conclusion coming from the application of such tools as chatbots, ASR or ASG in teacher education might be the understanding of the limitations of computers rather than the actual advantages – teacher trainees were amused hearing the English-language Text-to-Speach reader spell letter by letter "W Szczebrzeszynie chrząszcz brzmi w trzcinie" or seeing chatbots misinterpret idiomatic utterances. However, this illumination has led to increasing the awareness of the need for a human element in language teaching.

Jarosław Krajka
Uniwersytet Marii Curie-Skłodowskiej
Lublin

Dialoguing in curriculum development: On designing Information and Communication Technology training in modern philology setting

Introduction

The significance of educational technology, computers and the Internet, in the work of a foreign language teacher is not to be questioned nowadays. The dynamic development of new technologies, the expansion of the Internet in every single sphere of life together with a significant decrease in the price of educational software and office applications, all add a new dimension to the foreign language instruction, by providing the elements of authenticity, recency, variety, choice and interactivity to increase the effectiveness of the teaching process. Thus, in order to enhance language teaching a proper consideration of Information and Communication Technology (ICT) teacher training needs to be done in the context of official requirements for teacher education, as well as future teachers' needs when confronted with the technical possibilities they may come across in their everyday practice.

In order for ICT training to be systematic and comprehensive, it needs to be considered on a variety of planes, with a shifting focus on various competences and skills. With the existence of a wide range of branches of Computer-Assisted Language Learning (CALL), such as Internet-Based Teaching (IBT), Computer-Mediated Communication (CMC), Data-Driven Learning (DDL), Computer-Adaptive Testing (CAT), Open Distance Learning (ODL), to name just a few to portray the richness of possible applications of ICT in foreign language teaching, the reflection on the directions of ICT teacher training in the modern philology programme is necessary in order to tailor the instruction to the requirements of the Polish educational system.

The implementation of ICT training in the curricula of modern philology departments can be multifold. The purpose of the present paper is to demonstrate three possible approaches to curriculum development, and in each dialoguing and negotiation plays a crucial role – with trainees, with fellow instructors and with industry representatives. The paper recounts the process of dialoguing to arrive at particular ICT curricula.

Information and Communication Technology in pre-service teacher training – dialoguing with trainees

The selection of content for teacher training courses could be flexibly suited to the needs and expectations of learners. Thus, proper diagnosis of not only their computer literacy level ought to be made (in the pre-course test), but also a needs analysis is to be executed in order to investigate the priorities of teachers. The reconciliation of three indispensable elements of a needs analysis (Komorowska, 2005), namely lacks in the trainees' computer literacy, necessities coming from teacher professional development requirements (MENiS, 2004a) and wants as expressed by trainees leads to a successful training program. The necessary negotiation enables, on the one hand, trainer's better awareness of the computer literacy and practical experience of the group, and, on the other, provides information about the possible uses of ICT in their future career, to tailor the training to satisfy the greatest number of trainees possible.

The officially published teacher education standards (MENiS, 2004b) list computer literacy as one of the elements of teacher knowledge, characterized as "the ability to use ICT in teaching" (MENiS, 2004b), with the specification of the following four thematic areas for inclusion in the training course:

1. using terminology, equipment, software and methods of ICT;
2. ICT as a component of teacher's work;
3. the implementation of ICT in teaching a given subject;
4. humanistic, social, ethical and legal aspects of access to and use of ICT.

The balance between the areas above, and specifically the first three, will depend, to a large extent, upon the amount of computer literacy diagnosed on the one hand, and the clarity of pedagogical expectations on the other. The computer literacy of participants is evaluated by trainers in the pre-course test, negotiation with participants and observation of the practical execution of sample tasks, roughly corresponding to the advanced level of European Computer Driving License (ECDL) requirements in selected modules.

However, the content selection process cannot be grounded only on the trainer's preferences and trainees' expectations, but also upon the logistical considerations of the higher education institution. Thus, the pre-course work should also involve reflecting on available technological (type of equipment available, connection speed) and financial opportunities (availability of office applications and multimedia software), in order to approximate the content to the trainees' needs. Then, the items of the syllabus enumerated above should be selected flexibly, together with customized time allocation, for the ICT teacher training course to truly reflect the situation of a particular group.

As a result of negotiation, reflection and balancing, the pre-service ICT training at Division of Applied Linguistics of Maria Curie-Sklodowska University, Lublin, was designed to cater for the integration of both parts, the computer training module and the computer-assisted methodology module – for that reason, more advanced features of computer applications were introduced (e.g. word-processor's reviewing function, using the word-processor as a webpublishing tool or using email in subscribing to and starting discussion groups). With the increasingly higher level of computer skills, the component of computer-assisted foreign language teaching has been significantly expanded, to include the instruction in the following areas:

1. evaluation of Internet websites, retrieving of selected Web resources, copyright issues and webpublishing (Nelson, 1997; Krajka, 2002);
2. Internet-based activity structures: *telefieldtrips*, *treasure hunts*, *WebQuests*, *ask-an-expert*, *keypal exchanges*, *online research modules* (Harris, 1995a; Harris, 1995b; March, 1997);
3. the process of creating Internet-assisted lessons (Krajka, 2004);
4. setting up and running electronic exchange projects (Krajka, 2001);
5. synchronous and asynchronous Computer-Mediated Communication tools (discussion groups, blogs, wikis, MOOs) and their use in teaching (Godwin-Jones, 2003);
6. authoring tools, enabling teachers to create interactive or non-interactive language exercises (e.g. multiple-choice, cloze, matching, crossword, text reconstruction – Godwin-Jones, 2001);
7. using corpora and concordancing for language presentation;
8. computer-based materials development (creating PowerPoint presentations, recording and mixing online audio, authoring video, altering images).

The selection of areas for inclusion needs to be strongly connected to the actual teaching contexts that trainees already are or will be in. Consequently, the awareness of the available resources in the Polish schools of various sectors is essential. Similarly, the selection of tools (e.g. corpora and concordancers) is to be based on the availability criterion, favoring free of charge online access solutions at the expense of well-established but less accessible applications (e.g. *WordSmith Tools*), and building trainees' awareness of alternative tools (e.g. online word processors or Open Source office applications). Finally, an important provision for ICT training, itself the result of in-service feedback, is the inclusion of trainees in specialist Communities of Practice through learning how to use discussion groups and mailing lists (both passively and actively) and empowering them by gaining practice in webpublishing tools (ranging from website authoring, through blogging, using wikis to exploiting Learning Management Systems like *Moodle*).

Exploiting ICT training for core knowledge development – dialoguing with other instructors

In the alternative approach to Information and Communication Technology curriculum development, the negotiation with other instructors and reflection on other areas of core knowledge development leads to the reformulation of the role of ICT content in the overall development of a foreign language teacher/translator. Thus, in this particular view, rather than treat ICT knowledge and skills as an autonomous area of knowledge, with its particularly valuable aspects to be covered, the conscious decision has been made to select one particular aspect of educational technology, here corpora and concordancing, and incorporate it in the instruction of different subjects. On the one hand, this view follows the formula of a thematic curriculum (*program tematyczny* – see Komorowska,

2005), where the content of different subjects adds to the common theme, which here is the effective mastery, both passive and active, of corpus consultation procedures, ranging from using ready-made tools through exploiting the Web as a corpus to compiling self-made corpora to suit particular teaching/translating contexts. On the other hand, the training proposal outlined below can be characterized as a skill-based syllabus, as the trainees acquire various sub-skills of a particular area within the instruction of other subjects.

The selection of concordancing, and more broadly speaking Data-Driven Learning, as the core for syllabus development has been conditioned, among others, by some of the important issues outlined below:

- concordancing interjects authenticity (of text, purpose, and activity) into the learning process, and competence is built by gaining access to the facts of linguistic performance (Johns, 1988);
- noticing a word in several contexts extends the knowledge of that word and promotes successful learning (Cobb, 1998);
- corpora display greater diversity of language than coursebooks and dictionaries (Cobb, 1998; Thomas, 2003);
- knowledge encoded from data by learners themselves will be more flexible, transferable, and useful than knowledge encoded by experts and transmitted to them by an instructor (Cobb, 1999);
- sociolinguistic competence is addressed by drawing attention to the issue of register through analysis of actual language use (Krieger, 2003).

From the pedagogical point of view, the training can lead to the direct use of corpora in teaching (teaching about corpora, teaching the use of corpora and using corpora to teach) as well as indirect one (reference publishing, materials development and language testing – see Leech, 1997). Barlow (2002) defines and further describes three specific areas for teacher-directed corpora use:

1. syllabus design: conducting an analysis of a corpus relevant to a purpose of a given class to obtain frequency and register information to assist in course planning choices;
2. materials development: creating exercises based on real examples which provide students with the opportunity to discover features of language use;
3. classroom activities: hands-on student-conducted language analyses to elicit learner-made discoveries about language use.

Further didactic uses of corpora, conditioned by the type of corpus and particular purpose, are represented in Figure 1 below (after Gabrielatos, 2005).

The need to incorporate the question of corpora and concordancing, or more broadly speaking, Data-Driven Learning (Johns, 1988), the Web as a Corpus (Kilgariff, Grefenstette, 2003) or ad-hoc corpora (Zanettin, 2001) has never been put into question in ICT curriculum development. However, the vast amount of knowledge on various planes calls for reflection on the extent to which training should go. In this particular proposal for pre-service ICT teacher/translator training, corpora and concordancers have been made a major focus, with the coverage of both basic and more specialized issues in passive as well as active corpus use. What is important to note is that dialoguing with other instructors make it possible to relegate certain parts of training to other subjects, more

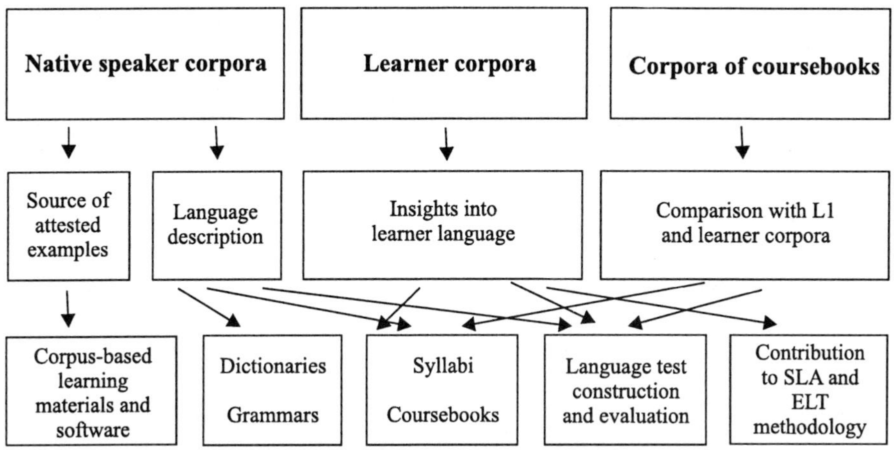

Figure 1. Uses of corpora (after Gabrielatos, 2005).

predestined to deal with them, providing either theoretical basis or practical implementation. When designing the curriculum for future ESP teachers or specialist translators (under gradual implementation at Division of Applied Linguistics of Maria Curie-Sklodowska University, Lublin, Poland), it was believed that if future language teachers are guided through the gradual process of acquiring concordancing skills as learners, it will be more feasible for them to undertake the same training procedure with their prospective students. Similarly, the training procedure followed by translator trainees will increase their language awareness and will enable them to find precise reference in customized corpora in their future translation jobs. Obviously, fair amount of negotiation, discussion and goal setting in the department is needed to make sure that the ICT training does really provide tools for other instructors to use. However, this provision is well-grounded by theoretical knowledge acquired in some other areas.

The training consisted of the following stages, covered either in an ICT class or some other class, with varied materials and activities, both for in-class and self-study work:

1. Introduction to basic concepts, definitions and taxonomies of corpus linguistics (*Introduction to linguistics*);
2. Using a concordance-enhanced dictionary (NetDictionary, http: //www.edict.com.hk/lexiconindex/) to expand vocabulary knowledge (*Practical English vocabulary/reading*);
3. Using ready-made concordancers (e.g. Online Concordancers, http: //www.lextutor.ca/concordancers/ or Web Concordancer, www.edict.com.hk/concordance) with selected texts to practise searching strategies and interpretation of results (*Information and Communication Technology*);
4. Using online concordancing interfaces to renowned corpora (e.g. The British National Corpus, http: //corpus.byu.edu/bnc/ or Collins Cobuild Bank of English, http: //www.collins.co.uk/Corpus/CorpusSearch.aspx) to learn about cor-

pus annotation and master more sophisticated queries (*Information and Communication Technology*);

5. Using ready-made concordancers (e.g. Online Concordancers, http: //www.lextutor.ca/concordancers/ or Web Concordancer, www.edict.com.hk/concordance) with selected texts to formulate and test hypotheses about grammar (*Practical English grammar*);
6. Contrasting the coverage of corpora (a literary text corpus, a representative corpus, a teacher-made ESP corpus – *Information and Communication Technology*);
7. Using a teacher-made ESP corpus with a concordancing tool to enhance the awareness of register (*English for Specific Purposes*);
8. Using a teacher-made ESP corpus as reference for students' personal language use (*English for Specific Purposes*);
9. Introducing learners to the procedures of compiling their own mini-corpora (*Practical English writing*);
10. Compiling custom-made corpora for the demonstration purposes in projects for particular classes (*Foreign language methodology, History of literature, Lexical semantics, History of the English language*).

In conclusion, it seems that what follows from the above proposal is that the incorporation of corpus-based language work should be done gradually, first exposing students to teacher-prepared ready-made concordance output, for them to learn to interpret the information. Once this is done, and once such crucial distinctions as simple search vs. associated search, prefix/suffix search, left/right collocates are grasped by students, they can be guided through concordancing tools with a teacher-made ESP corpus, to finally arrive at the awareness of the procedures to be able to search teacher-made corpora or personal corpora with text analysis tools. The other important feature of the training proposal above is that dialoguing with other instructors allows for close integration of the content, for some classes to provide tools and knowledge for immediate application in others.

Implementing ICT training in the translator training curriculum – dialoguing with the industry

Contrary to ICT teacher education, in which aims, competences and topics are precisely specified by the official regulations of the Polish Ministry of Education (see MENiS, 2004b), the area of foreign language translator training is not regulated in any way by any external institution. Both the aims specified in the graduate profile as well as the ways of achieving them have been the sole domain of the universities providing translator training programs in the foreign philologies curricula. However, mainly due to the predominantly humanistic focus of university translator training programs as well as shortage of modern computers and fast Internet connections, the role of ICT training, where it exists at all, has been severely diminished. Consequently, the graduates were often not provided with the knowledge and skills necessary to implement the elements of Computer-Aided Translation. In this way, the IT skills already acquired on the secondary level were subject to deterioration as well.

The specification of aims and selection of content for translator training courses needs to flexibly suit the needs and expectations of learners, thus, proper diagnosis of not only their computer literacy must be made (in the pre-course test), but also a needs analysis is to be executed in order to investigate the priorities of future translators.

However, the content selection process cannot be grounded only on the trainer's preferences and trainees' expectations, but is also conditioned by the logistical considerations of their actual translating environment. Thus, the pre-course work should also involve gathering information on technological (type of equipment available, connection speed) and financial constraints (availability of office applications and multimedia software), in order to enable smooth execution of training. Then, the items of content should be selected flexibly, together with customized time allocation, for the ICT translator training course to truly reflect the needs and interests of a particular group of trainees. In the curriculum described in the present paper, the analysis of possible areas of interest as emerging from literature was verified with translator agencies (so-called "necessities") and trainees themselves ("wants"). Thus, the findings of the research in the field as shown below need to be filtered through the learners' previous experiences, the possible immediate applications, the logistical considerations, the demands of the translator training program and the market expectations to compose a well-balanced course syllabus. The list below is by no means complete, and is rather intended to demonstrate a possible array of research interests:

- advanced word-processing as a part of the translation process: Pym (2003);
- corpora: Baker (1995), Peters & Picchi (1998), Uzar (2005);
- reference tools: Klimkowski (2002);
- discussion groups and mailing lists: Klimkowski (2002);
- Computer-Aided Translation and Machine-Translation tools: O'Brien (1998), Schäler (1998), Jekat and Massey (2003).

The ICT translator training at the Department of Applied Linguistics of Maria Curie-Sklodowska University, in its initial form, was conducted alongside teacher education in the field, with students not yet having taken their specialization. A 30-hour "ICT for teachers and translators" course was based on selected issues from the Decree of the Minister of National Education and Sport (MENiS, 2004b), adapted to the conditions of educating students in two foreign languages as well as two professional profiles (as teachers and translators). The syllabus focused on the implementation of ICT in students' work (dictionaries, corpora, discussion groups, terminology databanks, automatic translation tools), providing them with a toolkit of skills and competences that can be integrated in their present university work.

As can be seen from the syllabus above, due to the need to reconcile general ICT literacy (study skills), online teaching skills and computer-aided translation knowledge, the specific issues could only be signaled without greater development of the topics. Not sufficiently clarified student interests made the course highly general, and, in consequence, less immediately useful in translation practice.

In subsequent years, as following from the course evaluation and suggested by the translation industry, the computer-assisted translation component was expanded, by involving the introductory 4-hour training in one sample CAT program. Having taken into account financial constraints of the university, limited time available and the computer

Table 1. The syllabus of a pre-service ICT for teachers and translators course, Maria Curie-Sklodowska University, Lublin, 2004.

1. Finding, evaluating and using Internet materials for classroom use.
2. Web-based activities and Internet lessons.
3. Online authoring tools.
4. Corpora and concordancers.
5. Web dictionaries and glossaries.
6. Discussion groups and mailing lists.
7. Reviewing and sharing documents in a word processor.
8. Creating visual stimulus materials.
9. Computer-aided presentations.
10. Online course delivery systems.
11. Automatic translation tools.
12. Computer-assisted terminology management.

skills already possessed by students, *Wordfast* was selected to introduce students to the specificity of CAT. It needs to be stressed that the selection of *Wordfast* as a sample CAT tool served the purpose of exposing students to the functioning of such CAT operations as editing and managing TMs, creating glossaries, quality check options or reference/context search. Obviously, students were informed about other competitors in the CAT software market, with the most crucial similarities and differences highlighted.

The student feedback on the one hand, and industry requirements on the other, pinpointed the urgent need to greatly expand the CAT component, by providing much more specific practice of translation with the tool in a long-term perspective, at the same time clearly separating ICT teacher training from translator training. Once this was made possible by administrative measures, with the full 30-hour "ICT for translators" course available, the entire philosophy of the syllabus has been reworked (see Table 2 below for details). It has been decided that a sample CAT tool (here, *Wordfast*) will be introduced at the very beginning of the course and constitute the core of the entire syllabus, with subsequent classes expanding on its use and adding new functionalities. For instance, while learning to use online terminology databanks, trainees become familiar with storing terms in a *Wordfast* glossary; or while getting to know online corpora and concordancers, students are instructed in how to use context search (Translation Memory used as a corpus) or reference search (any file/s in a selected folder used as a corpus). In this way, a particular CAT tool serves to provide coherence to the course, at the same time enabling more effective Computer-Aided Translation in a long-term perspective.

Obviously, the organization of the syllabus makes it easy to rework it around a different CAT solution (e.g. *Trados*), once this is possible with logistical considerations. The training in another translation program will be inserted in class 3 and 4 of the syllabus above, while the other content areas (available as standard features of all competitors on the market) will be smoothly covered using a new CAT tool as a point of reference. In this way, a particular translation tool suggested or dictated by the translation industry is used as a backbone for the presentation and consolidation of ICT training.

Table 2. The syllabus of the "ICT for translators" course, Maria Curie-Sklodowska University, Lublin, 2006.

1. Searching for, evaluating and retrieving Internet materials for translation use.
2. Advanced features of a word processor – tracing changes and sharing documents.
3. Online machine translation tools – text, website, news translators.
4. Introduction to Computer-Aided Translation (CAT) tools – *Wordfast*.
5. Working with Translation Memories (TMs) within *Wordfast*.
6. Online reference tools: dictionaries, lexical databases, thesauri.
7. Terminology online: terminology databanks, glossaries, parallel texts.
8. Computer-assisted terminology management: constructing and editing *Wordfast* glossaries.
9. Online corpora and concordancers.
10. Concordancing options within *Wordfast* – TM context search and reference search.
11. Discussion groups and mailing lists.
12. Computer-aided presentations.

Conclusion

Dialogue, as an essential element of language teacher education, gains prominence especially when it comes to curriculum development. The complex interplay of needs, requirements and expectations of different parties of the process, such as the instructors, the trainees, the administration, the prospective employers, will need to be encompassed in a training proposal to the greatest extent possible. It is especially true in the case of modern philology education, where various career paths and opportunities will need to be addressed in order to provide graduates with the necessary knowledge and skills.

Information and Communication Technology has only been recently introduced into the modern philology curriculum on a par with other subjects, and much debate is needed about the shape of ICT training provided at the university level. As demonstrated in the present paper, the proposals may be multifold, depending on the underlying priorities adopted, and may range from independent training to a modular distributed course. In any case, dialoguing should lead to appropriate curriculum development, thus ensuring greater applicability of training to learners' needs and resulting quality improvement.

Bibliography

Baker, M., 1995, "Corpora in Translation Studies: An overview and some suggestions for future research", *Target* 7 (2): 223–243.

Barlow, M., 2002, "Corpora, concordancing, and language teaching", Presentation at *2002 KAMALL International Conference*, Daejon, Korea.

Cobb, T., 1998, "Breadth and depth of lexical acquisition with hands-on concordancing", *Computer Assisted Language Learning* 12 (4): 345–360.

Cobb, T., 1999, "Applying constructivism: A test for the learner as scientist", *Educational Technology Research & Development* 47 (3): 15–31.

Gabrielatos, C., 2005, "Corpora and language teaching: Just a fling or wedding bells?" *TESL- EJ* 8 (4). Accessed from <http: //writing.berkeley.edu/TESL-EJ/ej32/a1.html> (31 August 2007).

Godwin-Jones, B., 2001, "Language testing tools and technologies", *Language Learning & Technology* 5 (2): 8–12. Accessed from <http: //llt.msu.edu/vol5num2/emerging/default.html> (31 August 2007).

Godwin-Jones, B., 2003, "Blogs and wikis: Environments for on-line collaboration", *Language Learning & Technology* 7 (2): 12–16. Accessed from <http: //llt.msu.edu/vol7num2/emerging/> (31 August 2007).

Harris, J., 1995a, "Educational telecomputing activities: Problem-solving projects", *Learning and Leading with Technology* 22 (8). Accessed from <http: //lrs.ed.uiuc.edu/mining/May95 TCT.html> (31 August 2007).

Harris, J., 1995b, "Educational telecomputing projects: Information collections", *The Computing Teacher* 22 (7). Accessed from <http: //lrs.ed.uiuc.edu/Mining/April95 TCT.html> (31 August 2007).

Jekat, S.J., G. Massey, 2003, "The puzzle of translation skills. Towards an integration of e learning and special concepts of computational linguistics into the training of future translators", *Linguistik online* 17, 5/03: 41–55. Accessed from <http: //www.linguistik online.de/17_03/jekatMassey.html> (31 August 2007).

Johns, T., 1988, "Whence and whither classroom concordancing?", [in:] T. Bongaerts, P. De Haan, S. Lobbe, H. Wekker, eds, *Computer Applications in Language Learning*, Dordrecht: Foris Publications, pp. 9–33.

Kilgariff, A., G. Grefenstette, 2003, "Web as Corpus. Introduction to the special issue on the web as corpus", *Computational Linguistics* 29: 333–347.

Klimkowski, K., 2002, "The IT Revolution and the process of translation", [in:] R. Sokoloski, H. Duda, J. Scholz, eds, *Warsztaty translatorskie II/Workshop on translation II*, Lublin/Ottawa: Towarzystwo Naukowe KUL/Slavic Research Group, University of Ottawa, pp. 87–92.

Komorowska, H., 2005, *Programy nauczania w kształceniu ogólnym i w kształceniu językowym*, Warszawa: Fraszka Edukacyjna.

Krajka, J., 2001, "School partnerships on the Web – Using the Internet to facilitate school collaboration", *Teaching English with Technology* 1 (1). Accessed from <http: //www.iatefl.org.pl/call/j_article.htm> (31 August 2007).

Krajka, J., 2002, "EFL/ESL portal sites – an attempt at a comparison", *TESL-EJ* 6 (2). Accessed from <http: //www-writing.berkeley.edu/TESL-EJ/ej22/m1.html> (31 August 2007).

Krajka, J., 2004, "Creating Internet-based lessons", *CALL Review, The Journal of the Computer SIG* October 2004: 25–32.

Krieger, D., 2003, "Corpus linguistics: What it is and how it can be applied to teaching", *The Internet TESL Journal* 9 (3). Accessed from <http: //iteslj.org/Articles/Krieger Corpus.html> (31August 2007).

Leech, G., 1997, "Teaching and language corpora – a convergence", [in:] A. Wichmann, S. Fligelstone, T. McEnery, G. Knowles, eds, *Teaching and Language Corpora*, New York: Longman, pp. 1–23.

March, T., 1997, "Working the Web for education. Theory and practice on integrating the Web for learning". Accessed from <http: //tommarch.com/writings/theory.php> (31 August 2007).

MENiS, 2004a, "The Decree of the Minister of National Education and Sport of the 1st of December 2004 on the teacher development ranks" (Dz.U. z 2004 r. Nr 260, poz. 2593). Accessed from <http: //www.men.gov.pl/prawo/wszystkie/rozp_308.php> (31 August 2007).

MENiS, 2004b, "The Decree of the Minister of National Education and Sport of the 7th of September 2004 on the teacher education standards" (Dz.U. z 2004 r. Nr 207, poz. 2110). Accessed from <http: //www.men.gov.pl/prawo/wszystkie/rozp_302.php> (31 August 2007).

Nelson, J.T., 1997, *A system for the evaluation of ESL web sites*, Unpublished M.A. dissertation, Moscow, ID: University of Idaho. Accessed from <http: //itp.innoved.org/~jtnelson/thesis> (31 August 2006).

O'Brien, S., 1998, "Practical experience of Computer-Aided Translation tools in the Software localization industry", [in:] L. Bowker, M. Cronin, D. Kenny, J. Pearson, eds, *Unity in Diversity? Current Trends in Translation Studies*, Manchester: St. Jerome Publishing, pp. 115–122.

Peters, C., E. Picchi, 1998, "Bilingual reference corpora for translators and translation studies", [in:] L. Bowker, M. Cronin, D. Kenny, J. Pearson, eds, *Unity in Diversity?*

Current Trends in Translation Studies, Manchester: St. Jerome Publishing, pp. 91–100.

Pym, A., 2003, "Redefining translation competence in an electronic age. In defence of a minimalist approach", *Meta* 48 (4): 481–497. Accessed from <http: //www.erudit.org/revue/meta/2003/v48/n4/008533ar.html> (31 August 2007).

Schäler, R., 1998, "The problem with Machine Translation", [in:] L. Bowker, M. Cronin, D. Kenny, J. Pearson, eds, *Unity in Diversity? Current Trends in Translation Studies*, Manchester: St. Jerome Publishing, pp. 151–156.

Thomas, J., 2003, "Extending vocabulary knowledge with computers", *Teaching English With Technology* 3 (2). Accessed from <http: //www.iatefl.org.pl/call/j_tech13.htm#aword2> (31 August 2007).

Uzar, R., 2005, "Korpus a przekład", [in:] B. Lewandowska-Tomaszczyk, ed., *Podstawy językoznawstwa korpusowego*, Łódź: Wydawnictwo Uniwersytetu Łódzkiego, pp. 240–267.

Zanettin, F., 2001, "DIY corpora: the WWW and the translator", [in:] B. Maia, H. Haller, M. Urlrych, eds, *Training the Language Services Provider for the New Millennium*, Porto: Facultade de Lettras, Universidade do Porto, pp. 239–248. Accessed from <http: //www.federicozanettin.net/DIYcorpora.htm> (31 August 2007).

DISCUSSION

Joanna Rokita-Jaśkow
Akademia Pedagogiczna
Kraków

Challenging the (mis)use of ICT

The article by Jarosław Krajka has been written very much in accord with what is in vogue in teaching methodology of nearly any subject. It seems the enthusiasm for the state-of-the art technology and equipment have been replacing the well-acknowledged and effective methods uncritically, to the point where the role of the teacher seems to be limited to materials/resource collector and software provider.

The syllabuses suggested for ICT training of pre-service teachers (and translators alike) seem to be very sound, well-justified and practical. They recognize the necessity of using ICT when performing the roles of materials developer, investigator, project coordinator, administrator etc. While I agree that a computer can be a useful tool for the teacher helping to save time and offering enormous opportunities, I believe too often it is handled without care.

My skepticism towards the use of the computers in the classroom is rooted in not so positive observations of some of my colleagues and students' accounts of their CALL lessons. First of all, on principle the use of computers should foster the development of learner autonomy, yet this concept has been widely misunderstood, which manifests itself in numerous and/or extensive homework assignments and little preparation of the teacher. Whereas if the teacher really wants to conduct individualized lessons, his/her preparation should be much more thorough than normally (involving consulting appropriate websites, preparing worksheets, etc.)

Secondly, since the internet is abundant in all kinds of materials, a lot of teachers feel freed from any preparation or even critical analysis. They download ready lesson plans, tests and other materials, offer them to their students often without preliminary rehearsal or thinking of their applicability to their age groups.

Thirdly, the wide accessibility of relatively free software changes many of the CALL lessons into "Do-it-yourself" lessons, where in fact the role of the teacher is completely redundant. So why come to lessons, at all?

Fourthly, computer-assisted presentations or lectures (e.g. prepared in Powerpoint) often exempt the lecturer from familiarity of the topic as he/she can just as well read what appears on the screen.

All the examples given above are just a few and few between from the observations I have made. Hence my skepticism towards the overriding use of ICT. Perhaps the syllabuses, as suggested by Krajka, would aid the development of better and more conscientious use, but to my mind the education of the teacher should begin with thorough background knowledge and reflective practice. A thoughtful teacher will find his/her way to ICT on his/her own.

Leszek Bajkowski
Uniwersytet Jagielloński
Kraków

Corpora yes, concordancing no?

I would like to raise two issues in connection with Jarek Krajka's article: (1) what to put in a curriculum and (2) how useful concordancing is in TEFL. On a practical note, diagnosing the actual computer literacy of teacher trainees is a must and the resulting average should be taken into consideration. My experience shows that the number of things trainees can actually do on a computer often falls short of expectations. If that experience is not unique, it seems necessary to practice "mouse skills" alongside teaching computer-assisted language instruction proper.

As to corpus consultation, granted that certain obstacles are overcome, it seems to have a positive contribution to make at higher level of advancement – including teacher training. However, corpora may be used in a number of ways. Referencing online resources (BNC or simply Google), for example, is very different from elaborate analysis of concordancer results. Concordancers are primarily linguistic aids, whose classroom application dates back to the time of early CALL enthusiasts, motivated by the idea of a direct look at authentic data (cf. Holmes, 1999). Today the Internet itself is a vast corpus of texts exemplifying authentic language use in contexts spanning well beyond the n-word "windows", while EFL dictionaries provide corpus-based linguistic information adapted for use by learners. Web-enhanced reading comprehension or writing tasks may offer a more efficient way to teach words, collocations, register and style. Widdowson raised more general doubts (cited in Seidlhofer, 2003) that I see as supportive of this viewpoint. We must also bear in mind that there is no research directly focusing on independent corpus consultation by significant number of learners: Thomas Cobb's study was the biggest and involved a little more than 100 learners (Chambers, 2007).

CALL methodology today is merely a set of guideline books and some problems remain unresolved, such as the choice and amount of material to be taught through corpus samples. More importantly, there is a question of autonomy, which I see as a prerequisite for any curriculum that is based on self-study and the ability to reflect on "raw" material. In other words, corpora access needs changes in the broader educational context.

Bibliography

Chambers, A., 2007, "Popularising corpus consultation by language learners and teachers", [in:] E. Hidalgo *et al.*, ed., *Corpora in the Foreign Language Classroom*, Amsterdam: Rodopi, pp. 3–16.

Holmes, G., 1999, "Corpus CALL: Corpora in Language and Literature", [in:] K. Cameron, ed., *CALL: Media, Design & Applications*, Lisse: Swets & Zeitlinger, pp. 231–270.

Seidlhofer, B., 2003, *Controversies in Applied Linguistics*, Oxford: Oxford University Press.

Magdalena Szczyrbak
Uniwersytet Jagielloński
Kraków

ICT for translators at the Kraków Teacher Training College?

Since computer literacy is viewed as an indispensable component of both FL teacher training and translator education, it should not be denied its importance in university curricula. In his article on ICT training and curriculum design, Dr. Krajka stresses the relevance of IT skills development to translator training. Pointing to the fact that no official requirements have been issued with regard to translator training in Poland, he presents an ICT program tailored to the needs of would-be translators at Maria Curie-Skłodowska University in Lublin, underlining the fact that ICT teacher training should be separated from translator training. Among the numerous possible applications of ICT in translator education, the author lists machine translation tools, translation memories, lexical databases, terminology databanks, corpora, and concordancers, to name but a few.

In my view, an "ICT for translators" course, like the one designed by the author, is a viable option and, therefore, it should be introduced as an elective course in the Kraków Teacher Training College (TTC). Regardless of whether TTC students – majoring in TEFL methodology – intend to become professional translators or not, the ability to use online translation reference tools may simply increase the number of options they have following graduation. For that reason, encouraged by my students, I launched an elective non-literary translation course designed for second- and third-year TEFL students, who welcomed the idea. As could be expected, among the things that they appreciated most was instruction on how to use translation reference tools. Understandably, they embarked on the course hoping to improve their language skills and translation competence, as well as specialist knowledge.

I truly believe that the ICT program for trainee translators authored by Dr. Krajka may well be tailored to the needs of the Kraków TTC students. Yet, whether the current curriculum is realigned to accommodate the needs of the competitive employment market and those of the students themselves, and whether any ICT translator training is introduced depends, to a large extent, on the resources the TTC can provide, as my enthusiasm alone does not suffice for the course to be successfully implemented.

Magdalena Szczyrbak
Uniwersytet Jagielloński
Kraków

A Sage on the stage or *a Guide on the side?* On student-teacher dialogue in the Web-enhanced writing classroom at the tertiary level

Introduction

That the advent of new technologies has permeated and reshaped almost every walk of life does not lend itself to criticism. It also seems apparent that the modern education system is undergoing extensive transformation in which the role of the student, as well as that of the educator are being redefined. Needless to day, providing new communication channels, Information Age tools afford new modes of student-teacher dialogue. Thus, classroom interaction reaches beyond bricks-and-mortar reality and ventures into the virtual world, which, understandably, can also be observed in foreign language (FL) learning. Not surprisingly, learners – empowered by supportive and responsive teachers – cease to be passive recipients of knowledge and, consequently, take on more active roles initiating interaction with their instructors. The article addresses the issue of constructive two-way communication that lies at the heart of modern FL instruction. The author examines the nature of student-teacher interaction in the Web-enhanced writing classroom and explores ways in which the writing instructor may stimulate students' cognitive activity and encourage them to contribute to a fruitful exchange of ideas. She provides examples of effective writing tasks promoting students' autonomy and reflection, and stimulating successful cooperation with the instructor.

Role of dialogue in adult learning

It was already in ancient Greece that the role of *dialogos* – a basic form of communication involving a conversation of at least two people – was given due prominence by the then progressive educators. Typical of Plato's idea of dialogue was the teacher's absolute commitment to individual contact with the learner, as well as his/her management of the conversation inspired by the communication provided by the latter. Needless to say, open dialogues were conducted in a partnership atmosphere, with teachers respecting their interlocutors (Ledzińska, 2000) and promoting their active participation in an exchange of ideas. Similarly, Confucius's words, dating back to 450 BC, "Tell me and I will forget; show me and I may remember; involve me and I will understand" were an invitation to two-way communication. In the same vein, centuries later, during the Enlightenment era, Jean Jacques Rousseau, in his work *Émile ou de l'éducation* encouraged educators to inspire learners and to arouse their cognitive curiosity, with a view to fostering their independent thinking and promoting their research skills.

Understandably, since dialogue stimulates reflection and involves one's attention, imagination, memory and decision-making processes (Ledzińska, 2000), its role in modern education cannot be denied its importance either. It should be underlined, however, that dialogue is possible only when the interlocutors listen actively to each other's reasoning and take into account their partner's perspective. As such, it is an important tool that aids one's continual learning and development. Not only does it enhance a student's sense of his/her own worth but it is also a psychological prerequisite for a student's development of cognitive and metacognitive skills (Ledzińska, 2000). The teacher's role then is that of a facilitator and moderator who initiates interaction in which the student actively participates and which he/she learns to maintain and manage.

It should be remembered, though, that shifting responsibility for initiating interaction onto the shoulders of an independent student is a gradual process determined by numerous factors. Among the conditions that may impede this transformation one may point to: students' intellectual passivity (brought about by years of conditioning in school) and the hierarchical nature of institutionalized learning settings, including universities. An open student-teacher dialogue is possible only when the teacher assumes the role of an impartial observer and advisor assisting students in their quest for knowledge and inspiring their research and exploration of the world. As Brookes and Grundy (1990: 68–69) rightly observe, transforming students' awareness and promoting their reflection require a change in their attitudes towards "the learning of how to learn." Thanasoulas (2002), on the other hand, recognizes the relevance of a supportive classroom atmosphere and a cohesive learner group to motivating students and increasing their commitment. Likewise, Edmunds *et al.* (1999), who discuss principles underpinning adult learning methodology, recommend establishing a pleasant learning climate that is based on "mutual respect, collaboration rather than competition, support rather than judgment, mutual trust and fun." The authors mention five basic principles of adult education including: leadership, experience, appeal, respect and novel styles (Edmunds *et al.*, 1999), arguing that these form the foundation for effective adult learning. Further, they suggest that educators should aim to honor adult learners' individuality and to let them experience a respectful and participant-centered learning environment. It is in this environment that learning can take place and in which learners' cognitive activity may be triggered off.

Finally, achieving constructive dialogue by the teacher and an adult learner requires that the participants establish what they disagree on before they explore alternative solutions. The priority, however, is to understand each other's needs and line of reasoning. Thus, instead of being a verbal battle, constructive dialogue entails cordiality and strengthens the bond between the teacher and the student. Yet, the ultimate goal is to stimulate students' reflection and to promote their spirit of inquiry, which converges with the aims of constructivist theories defining learning as an active process of the construction of meaning and advocating a learner's personal construction of the world's representation (Myczko, 2005).

Student-teacher dialogue in Web-enhanced FL learning

Constructivist FL education, with instructors acting as facilitators of the learner's cognitive activity and reflection, has come a long way from tedious grammar-oriented instruction, with the teacher claiming the status of an infallible authority. Perceptibly, *the sage on the stage* model is becoming a thing of the past, giving way to *the guide on the side* approach empowering students and motivating them to generate knowledge instead of merely receiving it. Warschauer and Whittaker (1997) use the above terms referring to decentred communication enabled by network-based teaching and learning. They recommend that teachers should become cooperative partners rather than usurp the role of faultless experts.

Referred to as "emergent" pedagogy, the new teaching model aims to shape independent and flexible individuals who will be able to take up challenges posed by the information society (Pelgrum and Voogt, 2007: 12). As a consequence, the traditional FL pedagogical approach, involving teacher-directed instruction, is being gradually superseded by student-centered education. In line with constructivist approaches, FL teachers cease to prescribe the form and the content of classroom activities. Instead, they increasingly frequently stimulate students to construct meaning and to create their own solutions. Students, on the other hand, taking advantage of new tools, interact and collaborate both with their peers and with their instructors, sharing experiences and seeking creative solutions to real-life problems.

Urged by the needs of the information society, modern FL teachers place emphasis on promoting students' autonomy and enhancing their collaborative construction of meaning. Here, technology comes to their aid. Understandably, apart from the obvious goal of developing students' language competence, Web-based FL learning aims to foster the development of students' ability to obtain, select, process and verify information, as well as the stimulation of their cognitive activity and research skills coupled with the improvement of their social and organizational abilities. Naturally, one cannot overlook the obvious connection between the classroom environment and authentic settings in which students are to apply the newly-acquired skills and knowledge.

It should be stated, though, that Web-enhanced FL learning does not eliminate the teacher from the learning process. Yet, it entails a change in his/her traditional role. A teacher who decides to incorporate new technologies into his/her curriculum is expected to act as a guide, advisor and coordinator of autonomous learners-researchers. Among the roles of modern teachers in "emergent" pedagogy, Voogt and Odenthal (1997 cited in Pelgrum and Voogt, 2007: 49) list:

- Using instructional methods aimed at stimulation of active learning;
- Focusing on learners' individual needs and interests;

- Active creation of the learning environment for students;
- Guiding students' cooperation;
- Active support of students' learning process (involving provision of feedback and stimulation of reflection);
- Sharing responsibility with students for their learning process.

In the same way, Warschauer and Whittaker (1997) maintain that "Teachers' contributions in a learner-centred, network-enhanced classroom include coordinating group planning, focusing students' attention on linguistic aspects of computer mediated texts, helping students gain meta-linguistic awareness of genres and discourses, and assisting students in developing appropriate learning strategies." The authors also encourage involving students in the negotiation of the course content, as well as consulting them about the implementation of technologies in the course design, which might assume the form of anonymous surveys or class discussions (Warschauer and Whittaker, 1997).

On the other hand, students are expected to become independent and responsible team players who can plan their learning paths and monitor their own progress (Voogt and Odenthal (1997 cited in Pelgrum and Voogt, 2007: 49). Also, self-instructional systems, including technology-based approaches, allow for students' contributions being a mixture of emotions, attitudes, values, abilities and strategies, as well as needs, interests, knowledge and skills (Dickinson, 1993: 62). Referring to Warschauer (1996), Benson (2001: 139) states that use of "computer-mediated communication tools in language learning leads to more student-initiated interactions, a social dynamic based on student-student collaboration, more student-centered discussion and a shift in authority from teacher to student."

It should also be stressed that Internet communication channels, whose role in the reshaped educational context cannot be denied, enable the sender and the receiver not only instant access to vast language resources, but also the swapping of their primary roles, thanks to which the teacher and the student – acting as partners and coauthors – may be engaged in a meaningful synchronous or asynchronous dialogue. And even though in the case of online communication one may observe departure from traditional standards of written language, as well as the overwhelming presence of dialogues and colloquial language, the possibility of the application of the Internet in FL writing instruction may not be questioned.

Promotion of student-teacher dialogue in Web-enhanced writing instruction

Obviously, Web resources may be a source of inspiration that enhances and supports students' writing performance. Student empowerment in the Web-enhanced writing classroom may be attained thanks to tools like Web quests, e-mail projects, blogs, tandem learning, podcasting, multimedia presentations or online videos, to name only a few. It should be noted though that the implementation of Web resources in writing instruction is premised on the idea that "learning to write" entails "learning to learn" and that students develop their writing and editing skills, as well as discover new knowledge and reflect on their learning skills. What is more, online networking creates an authentic context for writing (for readers other than the teacher). Not surprisingly, in online communication students tend to be more active than in the classroom and, as a result, without further encouragement from the teacher, they initiate more interactions with their peers and with the instructor as well.

Yet, on the downside of the unprecedented accessibility of visual media, one should mention psychological problems that are likely to arise due to the influx of an enormous amount of information. It is apparent that easy access to a great deal of online data will not necessarily lead to its processing into a student's working knowledge. Predictably, learners appear to be unprepared for structuring so much information and thus they are unable to transform it into experience or problem-solving skills (Ledzińska, 2000). It is therefore the teacher's task to provide support whenever necessary, and to assist students in harnessing the overwhelming technology (Warschauer and Whittaker, 1997). Hence, a writing instructor's priority should be to teach his/her students not only how to write using online resources (including dictionaries, style guides, thesauri or language corpora), but also how to search for, select and verify Web content.

Targeting adult learners at the tertiary level and bearing in mind the importance of stimulation of active learning and independent thinking, the author designed writing tasks involving the application of Web resources and promoting student-student as well as student-teacher interaction. Here, it should be stressed that at the beginning of the writing course, the teacher and the students negotiated the rules which they would have to observe during the course and which would facilitate their dialogue and cooperation. The "contract" shaped the reciprocal relation between the instructor and the students, and provided for their respective rights and obligations, enabling a dialogue based on partnership and mutual respect. It accounted for both the students' needs and those of the teacher. The author adopted the process writing approach with a view to enhancing students' awareness of the writing process and improving their digital literacy. The assignments included, among other tasks, writing a research paper based on Web sources, online collaborative editing of articles, participation in an e-mail project aimed at the creation of an online guide with links to Web sites featuring British and American social and cultural life, as well as creative writing practice. The discussed writing tasks have been originally described by Czernek (in press). The most important information concerning the tasks, i.e. procedure, teacher's and students' roles as well student-teacher interaction are presented in Table 1.

Since it seems evident that university students should be able to independently examine, verify, and assess source materials, the author asked her students to write, relying on Web sources, a research paper about a controversial person. However, in order to raise the students' awareness of the writing and editing process, she asked them to submit completed papers together with annotated source materials which they used to support their line of argument. The students were to indicate the parts of the texts which they paraphrased, summarized or quoted (using the letters P, S, and Q, accordingly). During one-to-one consultations, the teacher provided feedback on the choices made by the students and stimulated their reflection, encouraging them to re-read the primary sources as well as their own texts. She pointed to the students' strengths and, at the same time, suggested areas for improvement. It is worth underlining that the task enabled the

Table 1. Selected Web-based writing tasks promoting student-teacher dialogue.

Description of Writing Task 1	**Online editing of an article (collaborative writing)** Students write the first drafts of their articles and post them on the university e-learning platform that can be accessed only by the writing course participants. The teacher verifies the first drafts and adds comments, adding links to relevant Web sites, where students can find information that will help them improve the form and the content of their articles. Students create the second drafts and post them on the platform, so that other students could provide their feedback and suggest improvements. The authors of the second drafts analyse feedback from other students and edit their texts prior to the submission of the third drafts to the teacher. The teacher verifies, edits, and evaluates the articles and posts their final versions on the platform in an area that can be accessed by all university students.
Web resources	– university e-learning platform
Teacher's role	– increases students' awareness of the writing process; – provides pre-text feedback; – verifies and edits students' final products.
Students' role	– provide online feedback on other students' writing; – revise and edit their own articles; – submit revised versions of their articles.
Type of student--teacher interaction	– asynchronous

Description of Writing Task 2	**Writing a research paper** Students select a controversial person (fictitious or real) and formulate a thesis statement related to this person. Students write a research paper based on a variety of reliable Web sources, trying to substantiate their argument. Students submit their final product (revised research paper) together with the source materials which they used to defend their thesis statements. In the source materials, students indicate which parts of the texts were summarised in their research papers, which were paraphrased and which were quoted (using the letters S, P or Q, respectively).
Web resources	– Web sites selected by students
Teacher's role	– verifies the final product; – assesses the selection of Web resources and the manner in which they were used in the research paper; – provides feedback (face-to-face communication with students).
Students' role	– search for, and verify the reliability of relevant Web resources; – write a research paper in which they defend their thesis statements; – submit the final product and annotated source materials.
Type of student--teacher interaction	– synchronous – asynchronous

Description of Writing Task 3	**E-mail project – creation of an online "British and American Studies Guide"** Students create an online guide with links to Web resources providing information on British and American life and institutions. The guide is to contain links to, and brief reviews of the recommended Web sites. The teacher provides a list with topics to students and the latter decide themselves who is going to find which resources. Students work in groups of two or three and cooperate by exchanging e-mails. The groups e-mail their draft reviews to members of the other groups and receive feedback from other students who suggest improvements and edit other students' reviews. At the same time, they provide feedback on other students' writing. Eventually, students submit the final version of their reviews to the group leaders, who e-mail the final version of the whole guide to the teacher. Students' work results in the creation of an online guide with Web resources for students who wish to find information on British and American life and institutions. Following students' completion of the project, students fill in questionnaires on their participation in the project, in which they perform self-evaluation and in which they share their experiences and recommendations for future project participants. Students also take part in a discussion concluding the project.
Web resources	– students' e-mail accounts; – Web sites selected by students.
Teacher's role	– initiates the writing task (provides students with topics); – provides support, guidance and encouragement; – verifies, edits and assesses the final product (online guide created by students); – stimulates students' reflection.
Students' role	– organise and divide their work; – cooperate with other students; – submit the final product to the teacher.
Type of student-teacher interaction	– asynchronous

students both to select the topics and to explore the lives of people who fascinated or intrigued them. The teacher's role consisted in initiating the writing task, guiding the students' Web exploration and, finally, assessing the selection of source materials and the manner in which the students incorporated them into their own writing. She attempted to act like *a guide on the side* rather than a critical judge, interacting with students in face-to-face communication, as well as providing feedback via e-mail.

Another example of student-teacher cooperation advocated by the author was that of online collaborative editing. Here, the students posted the first drafts of their articles on the university e-learning platform, so that other course participants could access and peer review their work. Additionally, the teacher provided feedback, adding her comments with links to useful Web sites, where the authors could find relevant information regarding the content of their articles or writing techniques. Eventually, improved versions of the articles were made generally available online. It should be noted that by participating in collaborative editing and peer reviewing, the students learnt to view writing as a process involving revision and verification of their original ideas. Noticeably, the teacher aimed to facilitate the students' writing and to provide support, where needed. In addition, the author promoted asynchronous student-student interaction by initiating an e-mail project. Also in this writing assignment, the participants peer reviewed their texts, by exchanging e-mails, and learned how to cooperate with other student-writers. Surprisingly, they seemed to have difficulty organizing their cooperation and dividing work among themselves. Still, the teacher refrained from interfering with the organizational aspects of the project. Instead, she encouraged student-student dialogue and assessed its outcome.

Last but not least comes creative writing, which, as the author firmly believes, should be included, alongside academic writing, in the curriculum at the tertiary level. Naturally, thanks to creative situations initiated by the writing instructor, students learn how to be assertive, nonconformist and unconventional. As a result, they become more open-minded and ready to accept "otherness" in writing expression. Related to the above are, understandably, abstract thinking, intrinsic motivation and a sense of one's worth. As can be expected, building a creative environment in the writing classroom depends on the attitude of teachers themselves: their resourcefulness, flexibility, and willingness to enter into dialogue with students, as well as readiness to accommodate their needs.

To help students unleash their creative writing potential and to inspire them to experiment with the written word, the author provided her students with incentives for expressive writing. Creative writing tasks included, for instance, writing poems inspired by visual stimuli, key words or a song. In addition, the students were encouraged to post their poems on a Web site promoting novice writers' prose and poetry (www.fictionpress.com). In the case of another creative writing assignment, the students were expected to read excerpts from modern fiction (downloaded from online libraries) and then to select a character with which they were "to conduct" a fictitious interview or whose "reflections" they were supposed to describe in a fictitious diary. Even though most of the student-writers enjoyed creative writing classes, some appeared skeptical, as they feared that their texts might be laughed at by the teacher or other students. Still, thanks to expressive writing assignments, the students tried to express authentic emotions and shared them with the teacher, which, in consequence, created a stronger student-teacher bond.

Conclusion

As has been shown, the Web offers many possibilities of enhancing FL teaching, including writing instruction. Perceptibly, Web-based learning results from the interplay between teacher, learner, content and materials. Yet, its effectiveness depends not only on the learning infrastructure, but also on the personal characteristics of the instructor and the learners, and, finally, their interaction. Needless to say, the availability of Web resources does not automatically change the educational content or the roles of the actors taking part in the learning process. Conversely, the potential of the new learning infrastructure may be fully used only in the case of a transfer of teachers' and students' traditional roles and a change in the form of student-teacher dialogue. Authors like Pelgrum and Voogt (2007: 13) aptly observe that information era pedagogy, as opposed to industrial era education, targets student-directed productive learning, cooperation of heterogeneous groups and peer support. Similarly, Warschauer and Whittaker (1997) recognize the importance of integration and networking, and of ongoing consultations with students.

In view of the above, the author's approach to writing instruction offered the students a chance to assume more responsibility for their learning process and to develop their writing as well as study skills. It converged with the postulates of educators who advocate using writing instruction for encouraging students' capacity for reflection, teaching critical thinking and developing competences that are necessary in the information society. Hence, the author's role was that of a coordinator and facilitator, whereas the students were encouraged to analyze and synthesize input material, to do research and explore Web resources, to solve real-life problems by collaborating with peers and, finally, to monitor their own writing and to perform self-assessment. All things considered, the tasks undeniably helped the course participants to shed their inhibitions and to become more autonomous writers. With time, the author observed a visible change in their attitudes, which filled her with enthusiasm and encouraged her to continue her dialogue with students.

Yet, it should be pointed out that implementing new tools in the writing classroom requires that the course design and the teaching methods be remodeled and that student-teacher interaction be reshaped. Inevitably, with modern teachers losing their status of know-it-all experts and shifting more responsibility onto students, the *sage on the stage* scenario will have to give way to the *guide on the side* model. It also seems likely that student-teacher dialogue will evolve into students' multilateral interaction with instructors, learning materials and educational technologies. However, whether technology improves students' writing and editing skills, and the quality of student-teacher communication will depend primarily on the manner in which information society tools are implemented in FL instruction.

Bibliography

Benson, P., 2001, *Teaching and Researching Autonomy in Language Learning*, London: Longman.

Brookes, A., P. Grundy, 1990, *Writing for Study Purposes. A Teacher's Guide to Developing Individual Writing Sskills*, Cambridge: Cambridge University Press.

Czernek, M., (in press) "Wykorzystanie Internetu na zajęciach z pisania na studiach neofilologicznych." Paper delivered at the conference *Rola akademickich ośrodków nauczania języków obcych i języka polskiego w tworzeniu europejskiej przestrzeni szkolnictwa wyższego* organised by Studium Języków Obcych Politechniki Wrocławskiej and held in Wrocław on 21–23 September 2007.

Dickinson, L., 1993, *Self-instruction in language learning*, Cambridge, New York: Press Syndicate of the University of Cambridge.

Edmunds, Ch., K. Lowe, M. Murray, A. Seymour, 1999, "The Ultimate Educator". Accessed through <http: //www.ojp.usdoj.gov/ovc/assist/educator/files/asciich3.txt> (9 September 2007).

Ledzińska, M., 2000, "Dialog w nauczaniu a perspektywy rozwoju", [in:] *Konspekt* 3. Accessed through <http: //www.wsp.krakow.pl/konspekt/konspekt3/ledzinska.html> (9 September 2007).

Myczko, K., 2005, "Aktywizacja ucznia w dydaktyce języka obcego: podstawy teoretyczne", [in:] K. Karpińska-Szaj, ed., *Nauka języków obcych w dobie integracji europejskiej*, Łask, Oficyna Wydawnicza Leksem, pp. 229–239.

Pelgrum, W.J., J.M. Voogt, 2007, "Innovative Didactics via Web-based learning: An Introduction". Accessed through <http: //62.44.100.87/wad/pl> (6 August 2007).

Thanasoulas, D., 2002, "Motivation and motivating in the foreign language classroom". Accessed through <http: //iteslj.org/Articles/Thanasoulas-Motivation.html> (6 December 2007).

Voogt, J.M., L.E. Odenthal, 1997, *Emergent practices geportretteerd: Conceptueel raamwerk [Portrait of emergent practices: Conceptual Framework]*, Enschede: University of Twente, [in:] W.J. Pelgrum, J.M. Voogt, 2007, "Innovative Didactics via Web-based learning: An Introduction". Accessed through <http: //62.44.100.87/wad/pl> (6 August 2007).

Warschauer, M., 1996, "Computer-assisted language learning: an introduction", [in:] P. Benson, 2001, *Teaching and Researching Autonomy in Language Leaning*, London: Longman.

Warschauer, M., P.E. Whittaker, 1997, "The Internet for English Teaching: Guidelines for Teachers", *The Internet TESL Journal*, Vol. III, No. 10. Accessed through <http: //iteslj.org/Articles/Warschauer-Internet.html> (4 November 2007).

DISCUSSION

Vita Kalnberzina
Riga University
Latvia

Writing in the world of transactional communication

Writing has traditionally been seen as a solitary activity, where we silently transfer our ideas onto white sheets of paper or screen. The process is *linear*: we encode ideas into words, these are written down one after another, forming lines, which the reader will decode again in a linear manner. Sociologists call this a linear communication model.

With the changes in our understanding of the processes of information processing, we started seeing communication as interaction, and we understood that if we wanted our learners to become successful writers, we should treat writing not as a product, but as a process. We would need prewriting activities where the writing process would start with talking, the students would exchange their ideas, form plans together, sometimes even present their paper before writing it. The end product of the writing project would nevertheless be a text written on a paper and owned by the authors.

At present most of us are part not only of the real world but also of the virtual world, where communication is not only an exchange of information, but has become an active force that can shape both the contents and the form of the text. We can publicize our ideas about the text to be written, our readers will respond and their reaction will affect us while we write the text. It is quite possible that having read the audiences' reactions we will write a completely different text than we first intended. Here we can see the transactional communication model where communication is not only interaction between several parties, but becomes an actor itself that will have the final say of the end product. It is sometimes not the fact itself that we have accomplished something that is important, but the fact that it has been communicated to everybody.

Magdalena Szczyrbak's article with the rhyming title *Sage on the stage or Guide on the side* explores the role of the teacher in the world of transactional communication, from the very beginning, i.e. setting the task, providing the students with support so that they do not get lost in the sea of information and finally assessing not only the students' written text but also their role in the process of their peers' text creation. However, this seems to be only one of the messages of the author. Beneath it we can see another, much more fundamental finding – although the technology has changed, the human thinking and learning processes are the same. When teaching, we will still need to proceed from the known to the unknown and follow the constructivist theories in organizing the learning process, we will still need to motivate our students by involving them in the process of knowledge creation, just like Confucius suggested thousands of years ago.

Agnieszka Nowicka
Instytut Lingwistyki Stosowanej
Uniwersytet im. Adama Mickiewicza
Poznań

Does web-enhanced learning mean new didactic relations?

The web opens up the possibilities of new ways of learning, and as each new tool or set of tools, to paraphrase Vygotsky's idea, it is both the expression of new ways of thinking and at the same time further modifies our thinking. Let us, however, focus on one aspect of "network for learning" that is communication. Since network opens new communication venues, and as a large part of learning takes place in interaction so also the contexts of learning in the interaction change. The web enriches our ways of communicating, apparently making them more accessible and diversified, adding more possible and more varied communication partners and new ways of interacting such as chatting, discussion lists, communicators, WEB2 communities of bloggers, that is the ones more option filled, in which users can influence the actual content and functioning of their and other people's blogs etc.

Putting aside the issue of communication universals, it seems that the predominating trend now in developing internet communication has so far been based on imitating the already familiarized interaction modes. Internet communication resembled the ways of interacting people already got used to, such as telephone communication, using the library, reading the newspaper, writing a message, a letter or a fax, playing a multiplayer game whose world is the simulacrum or gives the illusions of the so called physical reality (games' physics engines imitating the laws of physics in the real world, film-like quality of 3D graphics). However, the nature of the media (changing technical possibilities as well as limitations) does not allow for such a complete imitation of "everyday, familiar communication" so those new modes of communicating via internet tend to develop their own discourses and genres which might at first be challenging for inexperienced users but which consequently should become the new possible object and at the same time context of learning.

I would not exaggerate the importance of technical skills in using the new tool. Especially since the programs' interfaces tend to become more and more flexible, that is user friendly for beginners and more open to manipulation and filled with option combinations for more advanced users. It goes without saying that certain amount of computer literacy is necessary to use those new communication modes, but learning the basics of programs and internet interfaces does not only lie in overcoming technical obstacles but more in accepting the new contexts of communicating and in finding some personal aims or just joy in using them.

Lots of our students already communicate via internet. So they need encouragement to use web for more conscious learning of communication in a foreign language and consequently developing communication skills in/via those new contexts. This also includes involving students in multimodal (another characteristic feature of internet communication) dialogues and polylogs between a tutor and a learner and among students themselves as learning platforms such as *Moodle* partially allow us to do. The internet can become a rich source of materials that can be tailored to individual learner's needs, if they know what to look for and how to find it. However, it is not that resorting to web-enhanced learning automatically entails a change of the traditional learner's and teacher's roles and relations into more autonomizing ones. For example, learning platforms can only be used as a repository of learning materials, enhanced electronic libraries and nothing more. And the tasks left there many a time happen to be just too well known structural exercises, only appearing on the screen and filled in by using keyboard, not a pen. Not that such tasks are useless, however, the fact that they happen to be in a an electronic form does not by itself change the ways of learning and does not re-define the didactic relation into a more autonomizing one. Chats, conferencing, forums of workshops based on self-evaluation and peer-evaluation tools can be just disregarded by teachers in such platforms. On the other hand, both of those ways of self- and peer-evaluation can also be used effectively without a web. To sum up, the main aim still remains the same. Changing the ways of learning/teaching into more autonomizing and thus effective ones still remains not so much the matter of technology in itself as the matter of agents, that is learners and tutors who make a conscious effort to remodel their didactic relationship in whatever context it develops.

Jerzy Krzyszpień
Uniwersytet Jagielloński
Kraków

Peer student dialogue in thesis writing: A possibility to consider

In her article, focusing on student-teacher dialogue in Web-enhanced writing classes, Magdalena Szczyrbak rightly observes that this kind of interaction has a long history in more conventional educational settings and activities. An evident example is the traditional process of thesis writing, in which the author and the supervisor are involved in variously structured interaction. From the modern perspective, the supervisor should be a facilitator and a partner rather than an authority, whose main role is to give instructions on the form, offer suggestions on the content and proofread the text to some extent. Since the student's passivity (of whatever origin) may impede initiative on his or her part, it goes without saying that the teacher's facilitation in the process of knowledge acquisition and writing itself may require different degrees of guidance and the employment of various techniques in the process.

In this connection one may ask a question to what extent peer student cooperation could be involved in the production of licentiate or MA theses as a technique counteracting student passivity. It is highly probable that some motivated students exchange ideas on their projects even without any active encouragement on the part of the supervisor. Thus, given the modern approach to education, could the teacher purposefully and formally facilitate his or her students' cooperation in that area? If so, the student-teacher dialogue could be supplemented with guided consultations between students working in pairs, with the teacher acting as a coordinator. The procedure would have to follow clearly specified general rules. One of them might require that a pair should consist of students working in relatively different areas, to prevent plagiarizing of ideas. Another rule would specify the mode in which peer comments on the contents and form are exchanged. A further one would determine the supervisor's access to those remarks and the manner in which he or she reacts to them. Such a procedure would definitely foster the students' autonomy, stimulate their cognitive curiosity and reflection, increase their involvement in decision making and provide them with a valuable experience of cooperation. Such student collaboration in thesis writing would also imply a shift of authority from the teacher to the learners. The supportive contribution of a peer student might even be acknowledged in the thesis by its author. After all, do not numerous books written by serious scholars owe much of their excellence to the fact that they were read and commented on by other experts in the field before going to print?

Vita Kalnberzina
Riga University
Latvia

Foreign language anxiety in test and classroom situation

This research studies the effects of test anxiety on language performance during the test, taking an intrapersonal perspective, i.e. looking at the inner processes of the test-taker. The findings, however, suggest that the test anxiety effects on language performance are negligible, when compared to the foreign language classroom anxiety effects, thus stressing the importance of the interpersonal dialogue in the language learning processes.

1. Theoretical considerations

Traditionally foreign language anxiety was considered as social and situational anxiety (Gardner and MacIntyre, 1991; Horwitz, 1986) caused by the language users' inability to express themselves adequately. Horwitz (1986) claims that the essence of foreign language anxiety is the threat to the individual's self-concept caused by the inherent limitations of communicating in an imperfectly mastered second language. Schlenker and Leary (1985) also think that the intimate relationship between self-concept and self-expression makes foreign language anxiety distinct from other academic anxieties. Applied linguists have developed several branches within the field of research of foreign language anxiety. They distinguish between:

1. foreign language classroom anxiety and foreign language test anxiety (Horwitz, 1986 and Gardner and MacIntyre, 1991);
2. foreign language test state and trait anxiety (MacIntyre and Gardner, 1991);
3. harmful versus helpful anxiety (Madsen, 1982);
4. language skill approach (Cheng *et al.*, 1999).

The four types are discussed below.

1.1. Foreign language classroom versus foreign language test anxiety

Gardner and MacIntyre (1991) developed a study to investigate the constructs of different types of anxiety. They used 23 different sets of questions to measure different state anxieties (for example, French, English and general test anxiety, audience sensitivity, fear of negative evaluation, novel situations anxiety and social anxiety). Having carried out factor analyses they found three distinct factors:

1. a social evaluation anxiety factor based on the questionnaire results that examined the test-taker's anxiety during the test of mathematics, English and two social evaluation anxiety questionnaires;
2. a state anxiety factor based on a state anxiety scale, a novelty scale and a dangerous situation scale;
3. a foreign language anxiety factor based on a French classroom facilitating anxiety scale, a French classroom debilitating anxiety scale, and a French language use scale.

Thus according to Gardner and MacIntyre (1991), their results suggest that foreign language anxiety may be distinguished from other types of anxiety (factor 3), although there is some correlation between foreign language anxiety and general test anxiety and state anxiety.

The interaction between language and test anxiety is discussed also by Horwitz (1986). She used the Foreign Language Classroom Anxiety Scale (FLCAS) to measure language anxiety. She found a correlation between test anxiety and foreign language anxiety of .56. This can be explained by the fact that teachers often use tests in the class thus creating anxiety among the learners; test anxiety combines with what Horwitz (1986) calls a threat to the individual's self-concept. This becomes part of learner's and later test-takers' foreign language use experience that will be activated every time the foreign language is used.

1.2. State versus trait anxiety

Oxford (1999) says that language anxiety can start in response to a particular situation or event (situational or state anxiety), but that it can also be a major character trait. It can start as transitory episodes of fear in situations where a learner has to perform in the target language, and ideally it diminishes over time. However, if repeated occurrences of fear cause students to associate anxiety with language performance, anxiety becomes a trait rather than a state. Once language anxiety has evolved into a lasting trait, it can have pervasive effects on language learning and language performance.

MacIntyre and Gardner (1991) see foreign language anxiety development as a process. At the earliest stages of language learning, language anxiety is not present. If there is anxiety, it is either trait anxiety, novelty anxiety or even test anxiety. Besides, anxiety can be different for different learners; some learners can have test anxiety as the basic component of foreign language anxiety, while another student's anxiety can be caused mostly by social anxiety.

After several classes the student forms attitudes to learning the new language. If these experiences are negative, foreign language anxiety may begin to develop. If they persist, it may become a regular occurrence connected with foreign language use. The student starts to expect to be nervous and to perform poorly. This causes cognitive interference and poor performance. As experience and proficiency increases, anxiety declines in what MacIntyre and Gardner call "a fairly consistent manner" (MacIntyre and Gardner, 1991: 111). In some cases, however, this may not happen. A student may, for example, get into a vicious circle where performance deficits can lead to nervousness and worry, which in their turn can cause decreasing levels of performance.

1.3. Harmful versus helpful anxiety

Oxford (1999) differentiates between harmful and helpful anxiety, although she admits that there is not a common view as to when and how foreign language anxiety can be helpful but there are many research findings about harmful anxiety.

According to Oxford (1999), "debilitating" anxiety manifests itself in the negative relationship between anxiety and performance. Oxford (1999: 60) claims: "It harms learners' performance indirectly through worry and self-doubt and directly by reducing participation and creating overt avoidance of the language. It can be related to plummeting motivation, negative attitudes and beliefs, and language performance difficulties."

Madsen (1982) differentiates between facilitating and debilitating anxiety impact. He claims that students who are anxiety prone will not be evaluated as accurately on stressful tests as those who are not anxiety prone and therefore he attempts to develop a means of assessing when the anxiety level of a test crosses the debilitating threshold. He measured the level of anxiety of the test takers on scale from 1 (anxiety allaying) to 15 (highly anxiety producing) and proposed that the debilitating threshold is 9 out of 15. He found that on one of the tests, that of Reading, the students consistently scored above 9 and therefore he decided that this test should be excluded from the test battery in order to avoid results that are biased in favour of students who are not anxiety prone (Madsen, 1982: 141).

Madsen's proposal that there is an "anxiety threshold" (9 out of 15 or 60%) above which the test biases against students who are anxiety prone would be useful if his proposal had been accompanied by some arguments as to why the threshold should be exactly 60% and not some other level of anxiety. Instead, he explains why the Reading test should be excluded from the test battery:

1. for the Reading test it was the highest as well as the lowest level of proficiency test-takers who marked it as the most anxiety-provoking test;
2. the reliability level of the Reading test was the lowest for the high anxiety group (.65), while for the low anxiety group it was .89.

1.4. Language skill approach

Saito, Garza and Horwitz (1999) and Cheng, Horwitz and Schallert (1999) suggest that what we should be talking about is not general foreign language anxiety, but foreign language reading, writing, speaking and listening anxiety. Recent research on second language anxiety appears to support the existence of language-skill specific anxiety (Cheng *et al.*, 1999: 439). They say that this approach to language anxiety as a skill-specific anxiety would explain the contradictory results of many studies, where anxiety leaves a positive impact on one skill, but a negative one on another.

1.4.1. Foreign language speaking anxiety

The concern with foreign language anxiety started off by mainly focusing on oral skills (66% of the most widely used instruments for measuring foreign language classroom anxiety deal with speaking, Cheng *et al.* 1999). Aida (1994) says that her validation of the study of Horwitz (1986) Foreign Language Classroom Anxiety Survey (FLCAS) suggests that there is only one meaningful factor, that of speech anxiety and fear of evaluation.

Cheng *et al.* (1999) also say that the results of their analyses of the FLCAS show high correlations between classroom anxiety and speaking performance. They conclude that what is often considered to be classroom anxiety is in fact speaking anxiety.

Hilleson (1996) used diaries, interviews, observations and questionnaires to research the causes of debilitating anxiety during foreign language learning. He grouped his findings about foreign language anxiety according to the language skills. He found that his students mentioned the following causes of speaking anxiety:

1. type of personality: some people just do not like talking in a foreign language;
2. tiredness: accent becomes more pronounced as a person gets tired and as the person registers it, this becomes an additional cause of anxiety;
3. many people participating in a discussion impose a speed of interaction which is difficult to comply with;
4. an attempt to speak correctly interferes with speech content.

Hilleson also found that speaking anxiety was not a constant phenomenon, as the students were anxious on one day and satisfied with their performance on another day. Hilleson suggested that role-play liberates the students from their anxieties.

1.4.2. Foreign language listening anxiety

Listening, according to Vogley (1998), is the most frequently used language skill in the foreign language classroom and contributes more to language learning success than any other skill. Therefore listening anxiety is especially harmful. Vogley suggests that teachers often prepare special tasks for training the speaking skill, but they forget that speaking cannot be trained without listening: before we decide what we are going to say, we need to understand what has been said.

Vogley (1998) suggests that listening anxiety springs from the learner's false impression that they need to understand every word that is said. In her research (using open-ended questions addressed to 140 students) she found that the learners mentioned the following reasons for listening anxiety :

1. 51% of the respondents blamed input for their listening anxiety: nature of speech (28%), level of difficulty (11%), lack of clarity (5%), lack of visual support (4%), repetition of input (3%);
2. 30% of the respondents were concerned with the process itself: inappropriate strategies (e.g. trying to translate word for word) 24%, lack of time to process the input (3%), problems to study for listening tests (2%) and lack of opportunities to check answers (1%);
3. 6% of the students blamed instructional factors: lack of listening practice (3%), "the test thing" (2%), uncomfortable environment, e.g. too small a group, feeling hot or cold 1%;
4. 13% of respondents blamed personal factors: fear of failure (10%), nerves (2%), the instructor's personality (1%).

Vogley suggests that to remedy listening problems, it is not enough to practise and hope that listening will improve with time. If teachers want to improve their students' performance in listening, they should also actively teach cognitive and meta-cognitive strategies.

1.4.3. Foreign language reading anxiety

Saito *et al.* (1999) propose that because reading is not a social skill as it is done privately and has an unlimited opportunity for reflection and reconsideration, it does not depend on a dynamic construction of meaning by two or more speakers. At the same time there are reading specific factors that can make reading skill more anxiety provoking than any other language skill: unfamiliar scripts and writing systems and unfamiliar cultural material used to illustrate the text. Saito *et al.* hypothesize that anxiety about the text will arise at the point when the words the student has decoded do not constitute a comprehensible message. This anxiety should be separated from the other language skill anxieties. The results of an analysis of nearly four hundred students' responses to questionnaires suggest that:

1. reading anxiety is a separate construct (as all the questions aimed at reading anxiety had good internal reliability) which had a significant correlation with overall foreign language classroom anxiety (.64);
2. reading anxiety had a significant negative effect on language performance;
3. reading anxiety level depends on the type of target language: in their study American learners of Japanese were the most anxious (mean of 56%), followed by American learners of French (53%) and the American learners of Russian (47%);
4. the more difficult the readers found the reading process, the more anxious they were.

Although Saito *et al.* say that it is difficult to determine the cause effect relationship in reading anxiety, they suggest that in their study reading anxiety was experienced as a result of actual reading difficulties in text processing rather than reading difficulties stemming from the student's level of anxiety. This, to my mind, suggests that during the reading process the learners are constantly evaluating the quality of their performance and that anxiety is caused by a negative evaluation.

1.4.4. Foreign language writing anxiety

Cheng *et al.* (1999) propose that the results of research over the period since 1970 suggest that writing apprehension has a negative impact on:

1. the quality of the message encoded;
2. the individual's writing behaviour;
3. writing performance;
4. willingness to write or take writing courses.

The authors constructed a special questionnaire to address writing anxiety and compared its results with the FLCAS (Horwitz, 1986) results. Their findings suggest that:

1. the correlation between the FLCAS and writing anxiety is significant (.65) but is not sufficient to suggest that the constructs are identical;
2. factor analyses suggest that writing anxiety consists of three separate factors: low confidence in writing English, level of enjoyment in writing in English and fear of evaluation;
3. the comparison between the speaking and writing anxiety constructs as interpreted by the questionnaire suggests that the writing anxiety variables were more highly associated with writing achievement than with speaking achievement;
4. writing anxiety scores had a significant predictive ability in relation to writing skill, but not in relation to other skills;
5. the correlation between the learners perceived achievement and their level of anxiety was higher than the correlations between their actual achievement and their level of anxiety.

Cheng *et al.* conclude that their findings suggest the existence of separate language skill anxieties. Point 5, to my mind, suggests once again that there is an intimate relationship between the assessment strategies and level of anxiety, rather than the actual performance level.

2. Empirical measurement of foreign language anxiety

The aim of the research was to measure the level of foreign language anxiety and its impact on language performance during the Year 12 examination in Latvia.

2.1. The test-takers

All the test-takers were graduating from secondary school. Out of approximately 2000 questionnaires received, 248 responses were selected using a hierarchical multi-stage stratification method (Dyer, 1997). The sample was made up from different regions of the country, and from different types of schools (specialised language schools, city schools, small country schools and boarding schools) to represent the whole range of proficiency levels and to preserve the proportions of the type of students of the whole country.

After being assessed and evaluated at the same time as the other school leavers, the selected test-takers' papers and questionnaires were separated for the analysis of the level of anxiety, and the impact on test-performance. The population was divided into the groups according to their level of anxiety and language performance with the help of Standard Deviation.

Table 1. Stratification of the population of the study

Groups	Name of the group	Number of students	Mean anxiety level	Mean proficiency level
Anxiety S.D. >1	A4	34	77%	53%
Anxiety S.D. 1...0	A3	89	62%	56%
Anxiety S.D. 0...-1	A2	79	48%	60%
Anxiety S.D. <-1	A1	46	35%	63%
Whole sample		248	55%	58%

2.2. Instruments

There were two instruments for this study: Year 12 English language examination results and a questionnaire.

2.2.1. The Year 12 examination

The Year 12 examination of English tests candidates' knowledge of English used for communicative purposes in an English-speaking environment. The students are expected to:

- Understand and appreciate authentic spoken and written English from a variety of sources in colloquial, informative and literary registers;
- Seek and convey information, express ideas and feelings in conversation, personal and analytical writing.

The examination consists of 5 tests separately testing the four language skills: Reading, Listening, Writing and Speaking and also Language Use. Each test consists of 3 tasks of increasing difficulty proceeding from more familiar to less familiar situations. Equal weight is given to each section. The test is centrally marked by specially trained markers' teams. The marking reliability is ensured by double marking of subjective papers of productive language skills and item analyses of objectively marked papers of receptive skills.

2.2.2. Questionnaire

The questionnaire contained 15 questions:

- 12 questions referred to anxiety caused by the test;
- 2 questions referred to the students' experiences during foreign language classes (e.g. being afraid to speak out in the class);
- 1 question addressed the issue of whether the respondents had discussed test anxiety during the test preparation period.

The questionnaire started by asking the test-takers to circle the number (1 to 4) that would reveal the test-takers' level of anxiety (from *did not cause anxiety* to *caused strong anxiety*) for each task of the exam. For each task the test-takers were also requested to state the reason for their anxiety. They were informed that their responses would in no way influence the evaluation of their work, but would help us to develop a better test next year.

2.3. Analyses of the data

The obtained data were analysed using different methods: the Standard Deviation for dividing the population into groups of higher and lower language performance; the Mean for measuring the changes of language anxiety during the test; Linear Correlations for establishing the relationship between different variables; and Structural Equation Modelling (SEM) to assess the interaction between the different variables that influence language performance (using covariance coefficients), mainly to establish which factor affects and which is affected.

The SEM method uses the following steps: the interrelationships between the observed variables are measured to establish latent variables and develop a measurement model. Then, on the basis of previous research, interrelationships between latent variables are hypothesized and tested until a good model fit is achieved. Here, to save the space I have included the findings of the SEM in the format of table (see Table 3).

2.3.1. The level of anxiety

The overall level of foreign language test state anxiety fluctuates during the test and follows the actual and not the expected task-difficulty level (the tests are expected to contain tasks in growing level of difficulty), with some exceptions (for example, unexpected task type or topic). The change in level of anxiety is more radical for the higher language proficiency groups; their reactions are stronger when they have an unexpected task or topic. The level of anxiety does not depend on language skill or the task type although the listening anxiety level tends to be higher than it is for the other language skill tests (see the table below).

Table 2. Mean language performance and mean anxiety levels

Task	Whole sample		Groups of different **proficiency** level		Groups of different **anxiety** level	
	Mean (%) of the task	Mean (%) anxiety of the task	P4 (%)	P1 (%)	A4 (%)	A1 (%)
Reading	48	54	45	54	76	35
Matching	86	41	34	45	62	32
Gap-filling	37	52	42	51	77	32
Multiple-choice	34	69	59	64	90	41
Listening	61	56	49	56	81	33
Gap-filling	65	47	40	49	72	29
Multiple-choice	68	52	46	51	79	31
True/false	34	70	60	69	93	40
Language Use	50	56	46	61	80	33
Multiple choice	62	47	35	54	71	28
Editing	60	55	46	59	78	32
Gap-filling	26	65	56	71	90	38
Writing	54	53	48	62	72	39
Email	69	41	38	47	61	30
Recipe	54	66	63	74	78	52
Diagram description	58	53	44	64	76	36

A1, A4 – groups of different anxiety levels presented in Table 1.

The different-levels-of-anxiety groups are not the same as different-levels-of-proficiency. Nevertheless the level of anxiety does depend to some extent on test-takers' foreign language proficiency level as the highest level of proficiency group has the lowest level of anxiety and the lowest level of proficiency group has the highest level of anxiety.

2.3.2. The self-reported causes of Foreign language anxiety

The self-reported causes of anxiety can be divided into three groups: test situation, foreign language use and problems of test design or administration.

In the whole sample "foreign language use" caused the largest number of complaints by students and contains criticism of practically all aspects of language use (vocabulary, grammar, spoken and written texts). It is the middle range of anxiety and proficiency level test-takers that complain about foreign language use the most often. Foreign language use complaints were mentioned least often in the lowest proficiency group.

In the highest anxiety group, "test situation" is the most often mentioned cause of anxiety and it is usually connected to comments on the test difficulty level and to respondents' own reaction to this.

Among the comments on the causes of anxiety caused by the examination design or administration problems, unexpected task types or themes are mentioned 3 times more often than all the other complaints. All in all, test administration and test design problems are mentioned as a cause of anxiety most often in the two highest proficiency groups.

If asked about the levels of anxiety in classrooms, 35.7% of students agree with the fact that foreign language classes worry them more than other classes even if they are well prepared and 28.6% are afraid that their classmates will laugh at them if they speak English.

The correlation coefficients suggest there is some correlation between foreign language test state anxiety and language performance, the highest being for Language Use multiple choice task (-.266), which suggests significant negative effect on the performance of the students. The correlation between classroom anxiety and language performance is also significant and negative for test-takers regardless of their level of anxiety and suggests negative effect on test performance in all groups of test population. However, correlation coefficients does not explain whether it is anxiety that causes performance deterioration or the other way round. Therefore we will use SEM, which allows us to see the cause of the negative effect.

2.3.3. The effects of foreign language anxiety

The analysis of Structural Equation Modelling (see Table 3) suggests that anxiety has cognitive basis: Foreign language test anxiety is indirectly caused by trait anxieties: classroom anxiety (.58) and test anxiety (.73). According to my data foreign language test state anxiety has an insignificant effect on foreign language test performance (-.10), it has half the effect of test trait anxiety (-.20) and has nearly ten times less effect than foreign language classroom anxiety (-.98).

Table 3. Effect of classroom anxiety effects on language performance

Test performance	Covariance showing the effect of classroom anxiety on language performance (SEM)
Reading	0.99
Writing	0.82
Listening	0.93
Speaking	0.79
Language use	0.98

Classroom anxiety has a significant negative effect on foreign language test performance and affects performance in all language skills (see the table above). It was strongest for Reading and Language Use tests, but test-taker performance was affected in all tests, the covariance ranging from 0.79 to 0.99.

3. Conclusion

The crucial question for a language tester is whether foreign language anxiety undermines test validity, which is the case if we are measuring test-taker's ability to control foreign language test anxiety during the language test. The findings of my research suggest that the foreign language test state anxiety effect on test-takers' language performance is nearly ten times smaller than the foreign language classroom anxiety effect. Foreign language classroom anxiety has become a trait and shifts the test-takers' attention from what takes place during the test to students' everyday experiences in the classroom. My research suggests that although students feel anxious during the test, it does not affect significantly their performance, therefore students get better test results if they have had a good working relationship in their foreign language classrooms with their teachers and their peers.

Bibliography

Aida, Y., 1994, "Examination of Horwitz, Horwitz and Cope's construct of foreign language anxiety: the case of students of Japanese", *Modern Language Journal*, Vol. 78, pp. 155–168.

Bachman, L.F., A.S. Palmer, 1996, *Language Testing in Practice*, Oxford: Oxford University Press.

Bentler, P.M., 1998, EQS, A Structural Equation Program, Multivariate Software, INC, Version 5.7b.

Cheng, Y., E.K. Horwitz, D.L. Schallert, 1999, "Language Anxiety: differentiating writing and speaking components", *Language Learning* 49(3): 417–446.

Dyer, C., 1997, *Beginning Research in Psychology*, Oxford: Blackwell Publishers.

Gardner, R.C., P.D. MacIntyre, 1991, "Instrumental motivation in language study: who says it isn't effective?", *Studies in Second Language Acquisition* 13: 57–72.

Hilleson, M., 1996, "I want to talk with them…", [in:] K.M. Bailey, D. Nunan, eds, *Voices from the Language Classroom*, Cambridge: Cambridge University Press, pp. 88–117.

Horwitz, E.K., 1986, "Preliminary evidence for the reliability and validity of a foreign language scale", *TESOL Quarterly* 20: 559–562.

Horwitz, E.K., M.B. Horwitz, J. Cope, 1986, "Foreign language classroom anxiety", *The Modern Language Journal* 70 (2): 125–132.

MacIntyre, P.D., R.C. Gardner, 1991, "Methods and results in the study of anxiety and language learning: a review of the literature", *Language Learning* 41 (1): 85–117.

Madsen, H.S., 1982, "Determining the debilitative impact of test anxiety", *Language Learning* 32 (1): 133–143.

Oxford, R.L., 1999, "Anxiety and the language learning: new insights", [in:] J. Arnold, ed., *Affect in Language Learning*, Cambridge: Cambridge University Press, pp. 58–67.

Saito Y., Th.J. Garza, E.K. Horwitz, 1999, "Foreign language reading anxiety", *The Modern Language Journal* 83 (2): 202–218.

Schlenker, B.R., M.R. Leary, 1985, "Social anxiety and communication about the self", *Journal of Language and Social Psychology* 4: 171–192.

Vogley, A.J., 1998, "Listening comprehension anxiety: students' reported sources and solutions", *Foreign Language Annals* 31 (1): 67–80.

DISCUSSION

Monika Kusiak
Uniwersytet Jagielloński
Kraków

Teacher trainees' comments on test anxiety

The comments quoted below are a selection of opinions expressed by the students of the Foreign Language Teacher Training College at the Jagiellonian University, who participated in the TEFL methodology seminar I conducted in 2007/2008. The students were asked to read Vita Kalnberzina's research paper and answer the following questions:

1. What is the article about?
2. What is the aim of the study?
3. What concepts are investigated? Enumerate and explain them.
4. What research methods are applied to investigate the main issue?
5. What is the conclusion of the author?
6. If you had an opportunity to meet the author, what questions would you like to ask her (e.g. about the research tools, the subjects of the study etc.)?
7. Comment on the article. You may write about the aim of the study, the research method or your experiences as a learner and as a teacher.

I hoped that this assignment would enable the students to practice reading a research paper, i.e. that they would familiarize themselves with the organization of the text and, after having reported on the study, they would be better prepared to design and conduct a similar study of their own. I also believed that the students would be keen to relate Vita Kalnberzina's study to their own experiences, which could enhance their awareness of factors that influence teaching and learning foreign languages.

The comments below are a selection of the students' answers to # 7. I am glad to see that the teacher trainees were able to reflect on their own classroom practice and develop a dialogue with Vita Kalnberzina. The authors of the comments are: 1/ Katarzyna Wilczek, 2/ Anna Mroczka, 3/ Anna Kłębek and 4/ Katarzyna Wiązowska.

Comment 1.

"The more difficult the readers found the reading process, the more anxious they were." I find this quotation relevant also to other skills in FL learning. Students' attitude towards FL lessons and learning a FL is the key issue. In my opinion, enthusiasm, and not being afraid to make mistakes, learning from both your mistakes and those of others, together with self-confidence, are crucial. Learners benefit more from the lesson and perform better when they feel confident. In turn, when performing successfully they are perceived by others as competent learners. This is why the teacher should be full of empathy and understanding and should praise even the smallest success of his/her students. All in all, when the teacher wants to teach something, he/she should not only explain different things clearly, but also look into the souls of his/her students and try to instill in them positive attitudes and the belief that they CAN learn.

Comment 2.

I do not have enough teaching experience to comment on a level of anxiety among students from a teacher's perspective, but being a foreign language learner myself, I agree with Vita Kalnberzina's conclusions. When I compare two situations – being in a foreign language classroom and writing a test – I must say that the former causes much more stress than the latter. When participating in a foreign language class, we are constantly exposed to the judgment of our teacher and that of other students, we are compared to other learners, who also bear witness to our weaknesses and errors. When taking a test, the prospective judgment is more "limited" – only the teacher will find out how much we know and do not know. Our peers are not involved in this process, and therefore the level of anxiety is not as high, even though the results of the test are much more important.

The author says: "teachers often use tests in the class thus creating anxiety among the learners; test anxiety combines with [...] a threat to the individual's self-concept. This becomes part of learner's and later test-takers' foreign language use experience that will be activated every time the foreign language is used." If this is so, we could ask the following question: would eliminating tests change the situation? Would language learning be more effective? A long-term study would be needed to examine this problem further. We could compare the foreign language performance of students in two groups – those who have tests from time to time, and those who never have any tests. However, in our school reality tests are unavoidable and it would be difficult, if not impossible, to change the situation. Therefore, I think that teachers should be more concerned with looking at ways to reduce classroom anxiety, which may lead to a more positive attitude among students towards learning a foreign language, and in improved performance.

Comment 3.

The findings of the study may help teachers shift their attention from a test-taking situation to a classroom situation, and to view the learner as a prospective test taker. Surprisingly, the results of the study indicate that the anxiety associated with a test-taking situation is not the greatest obstacle for test takers. It is the classroom anxiety itself. This anxiety shifts the attention of the test-taker from what happens during the test to their own weaknesses and problems associated with a particular language skill used in the classroom situation. In other words, a particular test task may evoke memories of a similar situation from a lesson in which the learner did not succeed.

Comment 4.

The conclusions were quite surprising as they showed that although students feel anxious during a test, their anxiety almost does not affect their performance. What is more, students get better test results when they have a good relationship with their teachers and peers in the classroom. I did not expect that foreign language classroom anxiety can affect students so much and impact student test performance to such a great extent. Another thing I found interesting is that in the questionnaires a lot of students admitted that foreign language classes worry them more than other classes, even though they are well prepared for the lesson.